Lance Ford brings a blast of fresh air and fresh perspective. *Revangelical* is highly recommended for those who are ready f———————ed and good-hearted diagnosis of what's————— evangelicalism, and a pre————————————ing the Good News it was meant

TOM KRATTENM/
Contributing columnist ———————— ne *Evangelicals You Don't Know*

Part personal narrative, part iconoclasm, part confession, Lance Ford's *Revangelical* challenges the entrenched idols—nationalistic, cultural, and religious—embedded in modern evangelicalism. Ford calls for renewal along the lines of evangelicalism's own primary concern . . . that of the gospel itself. A prophetic call to re-evangelize the church.

ALAN HIRSCH
Author of *Untamed*, *The Permanent Revolution*, and numerous award-winning books on adventurous Christianity; founder of Forge Mission Training Network

Here is a path forward for evangelicalism that integrates the best of the past (e.g., the missiology of E. Stanley Jones) while it innovates for the future out of theological integrity, not political correctitude. Enjoy finding nuggets of wisdom on every page, not, as all too often, scattered throughout like breadcrumbs in a forest.

LEONARD SWEET
Bestselling author, professor (Drew University, George Fox University), and chief contributor to sermons.com

What would it mean for evangelicals to get saved? Lance Ford carefully and whimsically considers what changes such an awakening might bring. His book *Revangelical* is an "alter call" for all of us who seek renewal in the church we love so much.

DAVID FITCH
BR Lindner Professor of Evangelical Theology, Northern Seminary, and author of *The End of Evangelicalism?* and *Prodigal Christianity*

What I like most about this book is its courage and candor. I find Lance Ford's careful but plainspoken assessments and exhortations very refreshing and welcome—in fact, needed! He offers sound wisdom that calls the people of God to first-order things.

MARK LABBERTON
President of Fuller Theological Seminary and author of *Called: The Crisis and Promise of Following Jesus Today*

President of Fuller Theological Seminary and author of *Called: The Crisis and Promise of Following Jesus Today*Lance is dealing with questions that simply are not going away; if anything, they are becoming more pronounced. The core of this conversation is not *what* we believe, but how we relate to others and how we communicate in the public square. Sadly, we evangelicals have come to act more like a political party or an angry tribe than the body of Christ. We are to be salt and light, lifting up Jesus, loving all men—blessing them. As I have worked with leaders all over the world, and not just Christian leaders, I have come to find that the problem is not our gospel—it's us. Lance raises the questions the world has been raising for a long time.

BOB ROBERTS JR.
Senior pastor, NorthWood Church, and author of *Real-Time Connections*

Lance Ford is a significant voice among a rising core of evangelicals. Deeply concerned about the integrity of the church's witness, he offers a bold yet gentle admonition and re-introduces the evangelical church to the concept of the Kingdom of God. Speaking directly to the heart of evangelical America, *Revangelical* sounds a clarion call for the faithful to re-embrace the gospel's roots and to let those roots take hold in their hearts, their lives, their communities, and the world. Lance Ford's prophetic voice is cause for hope.

LISA SHARON HARPER
Senior director of mobilizing for Sojourners; author, speaker, activist, and playwright

Lance Ford's new book is an uncompromising call for us to be rewired by the Good News of King Jesus in order to bring restoration and renewal to an exhausted, chaotic, and strife-ridden world, regardless of the implications for our priorities, our politics, or our pocketbooks. Inspiring and prophetic in the best sense of that term.

MICHAEL FROST
Author of *Incarnate*, *The Road to Missional*, and *Exiles*

American evangelicalism is in crisis. The problem is complex, but the solution is not. In *Revangelical*, Lance not only provides a much needed, thoughtful critique of present-day evangelicalism, he paints a clear picture of what it looks like for followers of Jesus to truly be the Good News people we have been called to be.

BRAD BRISCO
Coauthor of *The Missional Quest* and *Missional Essentials*

REVANGELICAL

Becoming the Good News People
We're Meant to Be

LANCE FORD

TYNDALE™
MOMENTUM

An Imprint of
Tyndale House Publishers, Inc.

Visit Tyndale online at www.tyndale.com.

Visit Tyndale Momentum online at www.tyndalemomentum.com.

TYNDALE, *Tyndale Momentum*, and the Tyndale Momentum logo are registered trademarks of Tyndale House Publishers, Inc. Tyndale Momentum is an imprint of Tyndale House Publishers, Inc.

Revangelical: Becoming the Good News People We're Meant to Be

Designed by Daniel Farrell

Published in association with the literary agency of Mark Sweeney and Associates, Bonita Springs, Florida 34135.

The stories in this book are all true accounts, as told to the author. Some names have been changed to protect individual privacy.

Library of Congress Cataloging-in-Publication Data

Ford, Lance, date.
  Revangelical : becoming the good news people we're meant to be / Lance Ford.
    pages cm
  Includes bibliographical references.
  ISBN 978-1-4143-9015-4 (sc)
  1. Evangelicalism. 2. Christian life. I. Title.
  BR1640.F57 2014
  270.8'3—dc23   2014016907

Printed in the United States of America

20	19	18	17	16	15	14
7	6	5	4	3	2	1

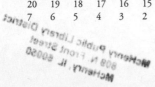

To my daughters, Caitlin and Amber. You taught our family the gospel by making it real in our lives with your love of others through unconditional acceptance, friendship, and openheartedness.

Contents

Foreword

THERE IS A WELL-KNOWN quote widely attributed to Mahatma Gandhi that continues to make the rounds online and has even made its way onto bumper stickers:

> I like your Christ, but I do not like
> your Christians. Your Christians are so
> unlike your Christ.

Whether Gandhi ever said it directly, or it is simply a summary of some of his thoughts, we don't know; to my knowledge, the true origin of this quote has not been found. But I do know that these sentiments have struck a chord in the hearts of many, many people.

Our culture has a very compelling interest in the person of Jesus—the Jesus who cared for the marginalized; who talked about loving your neighbor as yourself; who said not to judge others; and who hung out with both sinners and saints. But when we press the average person on the subject of Jesus, so often it turns out that he or she has never studied *all* of Jesus' teachings—such as when he speaks of judgment; of heaven and hell; of being forgiven only through faith in him and what he did on the cross; of not continuing in sin; and of repentance. Overall, the average person has a positive view of Jesus. But not of Christianity. Type "Christianity is . . ." into any web browser and you will see words like *judgmental, evil, crazy,* and *hateful* pop up. In the culture at large, the perception of Christianity is more often about organized religion, church buildings, and power and control.

Now let's take this a step further: How about the word *evangelical*? In some circles, to say you're an evangelical is even worse than saying you're a Christian—the extreme stereotype is that they're "anti-almost-everything," and for many in our society, this extreme stereotype isn't far from the reality of how they see evangelicals. But most evangelicals are *not* like that.

When I say that I'm an evangelical, I'm basing that description on the original meaning of the word, which Lance Ford discusses in this book. Evangelicalism was initially a refreshing middle way between liberalism and fundamentalism, based on the belief that the Bible is fully inspired by God, and because of that we take the teachings of the Bible seriously and desire to bring the *Good News* of Jesus to the world around us. I am proudly an evangelical in that way. The grace and beauty that once characterized evangelicalism has now been tainted by a new definition and impression. But the truth about what *evangelical* really means is still very Jesus-mission focused; and evangelicalism is still a vibrant, loving third way between other, extreme forms of theology that are out there.

There's really one way to change the faulty impression of evangelicals that some people have. It's not a new marketing campaign or a strategic rebranding of the word *evangelical*. It's simply demonstrating with our lives and actions the truth of what we proclaim. Whether we like it or not, people often make decisions about Jesus based on their opinions of the people who follow him. And there truly are some crazy-embarrassing evangelicals who fit the stereotype. But most of us don't! The simple beauty of the gospel, though, is that when we act like Christ, people see Christ in us, and the Good News goes forth.

If we care about Jesus, we will care about people. And if we care about people, we will be passionate, desperate, and motivated to share with them the Good News that Jesus died for their sins, was buried, and then rose on the third day to triumph over sin and death. That's what it means to be an evangelical.

Lance now shows us how to live out our mission for the sake of others. This book is a mobilizing book, a sending book, and it's full of practical ways for the evangelical message of Jesus to be heard and seen by those who don't know him yet. I am thrilled when I think of the lives that will be transformed as a result of this book. The more we embody the Good News of Jesus, the greater the impact on our society will be.

Dan Kimball

1
RECALIBRATE

*If I weren't a church leader or if I weren't friends with
Christians who really are following Jesus in a loving and
balanced way, I would probably judge Christians and
Christianity based on what I could see from the outside.
And it isn't a pretty picture.*

DAN KIMBALL

AS THE SUN SETS on a lazy summer evening, a handful of
suburban neighbors kick back around an ice chest on a well-
manicured front lawn. As Alan takes the last bite of a grilled
burger, his friend Brian—ice-cold beer in hand—motions
toward a moving van parked a few houses down the street.
"Has anyone met the new people moving into Jeff and
Stacie's old place?"

"I met the wife," Brenda says. "I was out running a couple
of days ago and she was getting something out of her car, so
I stopped and introduced myself and welcomed her to the
neighborhood. She was really friendly. I think she said they're
from Cincinnati."

"What does *he* do?" Alan asks.

"I think he works at a tech firm or something," Brenda says, before adding, "Oh yeah! And here's the best part. I was meaning to tell you all. They're *evangelical Christians*. She's got a Jesus fish and a pro-life bumper sticker on her car and everything."

Upon hearing this last bit of news, Brian gives Steve a high five. "*Yes!* That's *great* news."

Leslie, too, is clearly elated. "Oh man, that is so awesome!"

"No kidding," says Steve. "That is *exactly* what this neighborhood needs. Some evangelicals."

◆ ◆ ◆

Whenever I speak to live audiences and paint that scenario, the room—without fail—erupts in laughter. Why is that? Because we all know better. Who gets excited when they hear, "The evangelicals are coming!" The answer is *nobody* . . . except maybe other evangelicals.

Today, the term *evangelical* is a loaded word in American culture, packed with a variety of contradictory meanings. The emotions it evokes in one person can be the polar opposite of how it affects someone else. What *evangelical* is supposed to mean—*bringer of good news*—is completely different from what it has come to mean for many in our society: judgmental, misogynist, bigoted, homophobic. How did this happen? How did the "good news" people come to be widely regarded as *bad news*?

To answer that question, I didn't have to look much further than my own upbringing.

Evangelicaled

During the decade of the 1960s, my father, an accomplished guitarist, played in honky-tonks throughout the Dallas/Ft. Worth metroplex. Along with his love for my mother, my sister, and me, my dad loved country-western music chased down with a few beers. Actually, more than a few. Where most people might have one or two cans or bottles, my dad would have one or two six-packs. Daddy coming home drunk was an all-too-frequent occurrence in our home. The only things that kept divorce at bay were my mother's love for my father and her unrelenting commitment to keep our family together.

Sometime around 1969, the year of the lunar landing, my father had a health scare and wound up in the hospital. While he was there, my grandfather and his pastor visited my father's bedside and prayed the "sinner's prayer" with him after walking him down "the Romans Road."[1] Amazingly, it stuck, and my father got *saved*. And soon the rest of our household got saved as well.

Growing up in the Bible Belt in the 1970s meant that every school day began with the Pledge of Allegiance and possibly a prayer, led over the intercom by the school principal. At some point during the school year, we were certain to receive a little green copy of the New Testament, compliments of the Gideons.

On Sundays, we sat side by side on rock-hard church pews that were just uncomfortable enough to keep us awake while the pastor delivered the Word of God from behind an imposing pulpit, flanked on the platform by two important symbols—the American flag and the Christian flag. When the church service was over, we went home for Sunday dinner. In the afternoon, there might be a trip to the park or a lake, but we certainly wouldn't be going to the mall or the movies. Commercial enterprises for the most part were closed in accordance with the blue laws.[2]

As the 1970s progressed, the Cold War grew darker on the international front while a culture war intensified stateside. The ever-present danger of communism and nuclear war lurked in the shadows, tainting our innate American optimism with fear. We were convinced that the Russians could launch their missiles at us at any moment. Anything with a mere hint of communism was to be stamped out. Certain phrases came to be viewed not merely as opinion but as unquestionable fact to all but the most ignorant, unpatriotic traitor or communist:

- "America is a Christian nation."

- "America is the greatest nation on earth."

- "God, guns, and country" (or "God, guns, and Texas" if you were fortunate enough to have been born in the Republic).

On the home front, two major court decisions—the 1962 Supreme Court prohibition of organized school prayer and the 1973 Supreme Court decision legalizing abortion—combined to galvanize evangelical leaders around a handful of issues. Evangelical pastors and leaders began to speak loudly—and often—on a particular set of political and moral subjects. Abortion and school prayer became key points in a battle that would eventually create an identity and agenda for the majority of evangelicals in the United States.

For us kids, one week each summer was devoted to Vacation Bible School, where we pledged our allegiance in triplicate—first to the American flag, and then to the Christian flag and the Bible. It was clear in our young minds that we were to commit to, live by, and defend all three with equal devotion. I was pretty sure that when God sat on his throne, Jesus was on one side, with the American flag next to him, and the Holy Spirit was on the other side, with a Christian flag of equal size.

Sometime in the midseventies, I remember being terrified by the rapture movie called *A Thief in the Night*, with its haunting rendition of Larry Norman's song "I Wish We'd All Been Ready." Coming home to an empty house one winter evening, not long after I had watched this film about people who missed out on being taken up to heaven before the Great Tribulation (in accordance with a dispensational interpretation of Matthew 24:36-44), I became convinced I had been "left behind." My dad was working the night shift at the time and my mom was way past her normal arrival time after work. This was decades before cell phones, and with no way to get in touch with my mom, I grew panicky and tears began to flow. I climbed onto the roof of our house to watch in all directions for signs of life. I saw a few cars coming and going, but figured those were lost people like me who had been passed over by the coming of the Lord. Then again, I didn't see any cars going out of control or crashing like the movie had portrayed. Soon enough, my mom arrived home and my rapture fears subsided. Nevertheless, I didn't ever want to have that terrifying feeling again.

I couldn't wait to get to church the next Sunday because I knew exactly what I needed to do. Though I was just a youngster, I had gone to church enough to know what would happen following the pastor's sermon. We would all get "the invitation," followed by "the question," and then I would have my opportunity to get my ticket punched for heaven.

It was all I could do to sit still until the sermon was over and I heard the familiar words: "Every head bowed and every eye closed. No one looking around. . . . Now, if you were to die tonight and stand before God and he were to ask you why he should let you into his heaven, how would you respond?"

After the pastor recited a list of possible answers and why every one of them would fail to secure our entry into heaven, he said, "If you do not want to face an eternity of torment in hell, I invite you to signify your desire by raising your hand."

My hand shot up as quickly and as high as I could raise it. And then I heard the all-important words that the pastor had spoken umpteen times before in countless church services: "I see that hand."

Ahh. Sweet relief began to flow. *Yes, he saw my hand!* I then answered the invitation to walk to the front of the church to pray the "sinner's prayer" and accept Jesus as my Savior, as my parents sang "Just As I Am" along with the rest of the congregation. *Whew.* I was in. I would not be going to hell.

Over the next decade, there were only a handful of Sundays when I did not attend church services with my family. I became adept at finding my way around the Bible, and I developed a familiarity with all the key stories: Noah and the ark, Jonah and the whale, Samson and his great strength, David and Goliath, and so on. I knew the names of most of the twelve disciples and could recite the narrative of Jesus' birth, a few of his miracles, and the story of his trial, death, and resurrection. And along with other members of our church, I was taught that the most important issue of all— our number one priority—was to keep other people from going to hell.

We were given a few "tools" (mostly canned sales pitches) to help us in our evangelistic efforts to rescue people from eternal fire and damnation, but otherwise the "good news" of the gospel we learned was pretty much limited to "you don't have to go to hell." It was a message about what happens to us *after* we die. It didn't have much to say about what we might do *before* we die. Oh, there were plenty of expectations, both spoken and assumed, about what we *wouldn't do* (and every church had its list), but the emphasis was mostly on believing a few key facts about Jesus—his birth, death, resurrection, imminent return, and status as Savior—and then we were good to go. We were all familiar with the standard question,

"If you died tonight, do you know where you would spend eternity?" but nobody ever seemed to ask, "If you *live* tonight, how will you enter the Kingdom of Heaven?"

I have been an evangelical Christian long enough to know that what I've just described is a condensed version of the gospel that most of us learned. I may have overstated the issue a little bit—maybe a smidgen—but not by much. For the most part, the evangelical gospel has been reduced to a message that has a lot more to do with dying than with living. It has been more about "hellfire insurance" than living a life on fire from heaven.

After my salvation experience, and for the rest of my adolescent years, I took this truncated gospel to heart and pretty much lived as I pleased and chased what I wanted, with scant regard for the ways of the Lord. I fully relied on God's amazing grace to make everything work out in the end.

Us vs. Them

Shortly after graduating from high school, I experienced a Prodigal Son–like return to a life of earnest devotion to the Lord. I immediately enrolled at a Bible college and set off on a course of "full-time ministry." Over the next several years, my objective became clear: keep as many people as possible out of the fires of hell, but without getting smoky in the rescue effort. We called this "hating the sin but loving the sinner," but what it really meant, in practice, was that we distanced ourselves from any meaningful contact with non-Christians apart from our evangelistic campaigns.

The evangelical stream I began swimming in emphasized the importance of "avoiding friendship with the world," meaning anyone who was caught up in the "secular world system." In other words, your friends should only be Christians and only Christians should be your friends.

Something about this began to marinate in my heart. It was our duty to "love sinners," but we didn't have to actually like them, and we certainly didn't want to get too close to them, for fear that something bad might rub off or someone from church might see us. In fact, if we had too much affinity for non-Christians, it was indicative that something was amiss in our hearts. We were only to lower our guard and befriend people *after* they accepted Jesus.

With that mind-set, it's no surprise that, before long, I was like the average believer, who has no non-Christian friends other than coworkers or casual acquaintances.

During my first year in Bible college, an expert on personal evangelism came to campus and offered to spend an afternoon with students who wanted to learn his techniques. I showed up for the training at the appointed time and place, along with a half-dozen other students, and for the next three hours, we learned door-to-door evangelism strategies and how to jump on city buses to give one-minute evangelistic pitches leading to a ten-second countdown that concluded with a recital of the "sinner's prayer." We were instructed to end these brief gospel presentations by telling the new "converts" to find a Bible-believing church to attend. There was no relationship established—not even close, because relationship was not the goal. We would never see any of these people again. All that really mattered was being able to tally up "the day's catch," as the evangelist called it.

In the summer of 1986, fresh out of Bible college and newly married, I set off with my wife to serve as youth pastors at a West Texas church in a small junior college town. The church was known for leading protests and petition drives on a variety of moral issues.

Shortly after I arrived, the pastor took me for a ride around town, during which he gave me an orientation on which businesses to avoid and which restaurants were forbidden for staff members to patronize. For the next six months, we didn't eat pizza because the only pizza place in town served alcohol. I was well on my way to a worldview based on opposing categories—Christian vs. non-Christian, *us* vs. *them*. *They* could become *us* if only they would repent and believe. But unless and until they did so, it would be very hard not to look at them as the enemy. At the very least, they were in cahoots with the enemy.

By the 1990s, the issue of homosexuality had joined abortion, creationism, and public school prayer as the major focus points of evangelicalism. American society no longer treated Christianity with favored status, and the most noticeable response by evangelical Christians was to hunker down into political strategies and standoffs. "Restore America to Its Christian Foundation" and "Take Back Our Nation" became common themes.

By this point, I had been a practicing evangelical and

full-time ministry worker for long enough that, along with the leading voices of evangelicalism, I was galvanized into "us vs. them" thinking, attitudes, and postures. "They" were sending our great nation to hell in a handbasket. "They" were ruining our schools. "They" were killing innocent babies. This paradigm effectively paralyzed any Christlike love in my heart and dictated the way I interacted with, spoke of, and treated those outside of the evangelical Christian camp. Political or philosophical differences branded other people as the enemy, and they were treated and spoken of as such. Their outrageous views of life and society were not deserving of respect, and therefore they would find none from me and my tribe. I had become a fine young Pharisee.

During a sermon for a sizable number of college and high school students one evening, I made an extremely derogatory statement about homosexuals. It elicited widespread laughter from the gathering of evangelical young people.

Following the sermon, a young man named Jeff came straight toward me. I was certain he was going to congratulate me on the great message I had just delivered, but I was in for a shock. Instead, he loudly and summarily informed me that my comment about gays had been completely out-of-line and that I had the intelligence of a mentally disabled grasshopper.

I responded that I was in charge of the meeting and he was welcome to leave the premises as soon as he could locate an exit. As Jeff walked out, several people gathered around me in admiration for my "boldness in the name of truth."

Despite a steady diet of Bible study and considerable

chunks of time spent reading the four Gospels, it had somehow escaped me that the way I viewed and treated anyone
I categorized as a non-Jesus follower was nothing like the
way Jesus treated people who had not yet begun to follow
him. Stop for a second and consider that when Jesus began
his ministry, there were no Christians and no Christianity.
Sure, there were people who feared God, devout Jews who
sought to uphold the law of God. But by the same token,
there was more than enough immorality to go around. While
the Pharisees, scribes, chief priests, and leaders of the synagogues perspired over every last jot and tittle of the law
and conspired against the enemies of righteousness and of
Israel, Jesus consorted with, served, and befriended scores of
"unrighteous" people—scamps, scalawags, and sinners.

The Gospels are a compendium of Jesus' encounters with
the most egregious people, as to their immorality, corruption, and bad reputation. But somehow it seems that many
evangelicals today have chosen to overlook or ignore how
Jesus responded to "those people"—the *thems* of his day. In
case after case—in fact, without exception—he approached
them with kindness, mercy, and an invitation to a banquet
in his Kingdom. The people he got upset with were never
the *thems*; it was always *us*, the "good church folks" who
condemned "sinners" or created barriers between them and
their heavenly Father.

Jesus never condemned sinners. His issue was with people
who thought they were not sinners themselves. His gospel
eliminated the categories of *us* vs. *them* because it eliminated

fear—fear of others and fear of death. Jesus was confident that the God-life inside of him would swallow up any disease or corruption he might encounter and would overcome any death-bearing element he might touch. But this didn't set well with the evangelicals of his day. His attitude and actions toward the nonreligious elicited the wrath of the religious elite to the point that they eventually arranged for his execution. It's sobering to contemplate the way many evangelicals might treat Jesus if he were walking among us today.

Revangelicaled

When Jeff challenged me that night following my sermon, his response had nothing to do with whether homosexuality was a sin. The issue was my *attitude*, which was reflected in my words, which revealed my *heart*. There was no hiding it. None of that "my heart was in the right place" business. No, my heart *wasn't* right. My heart was dead wrong. Dreadfully wrong. Jeff confronted me with the truth that if the love of Jesus for others was alive or even existed in my heart, it had been buried under so much self-righteous rubble and a lack of understanding of Jesus' ways and means (as clearly revealed in the Gospels) that I couldn't reach it. For all practical purposes, I was untouched by the very gospel I claimed to be offering to others.

Something was amiss, and deep down I knew it. I wasn't at all like the Jesus I claimed to love. I began to ask myself some tough questions about how I—along with the majority of fervent evangelicals I knew—had gotten to the point where

I didn't actually love non-Christians at all. I loved the *idea* of their becoming converts (and was drawn to high-profile conversions), and in an abstract way I loved their "souls." But I would continue to view them as the enemy—rather than as sheep in need of a shepherd—until they became Christians. And I knew I was not alone. All I needed to do was turn on any of the leading evangelical radio talk shows or listen to any of the leading evangelical voices during election season. The prevailing message was to "protect yourself and your family" from the ungodly *others* in society.

Almost a decade after my encounter with Jeff, he and I unexpectedly found ourselves only a few feet apart at a conference in St. Louis. Glancing across the crowded room, we caught each other's eyes, but this time, *I* was the one who made a beeline straight to *him*. As Jeff steeled himself for what would surely be an awkward or confrontational moment, I took him completely off guard with my first words.

"I was wrong," I said emphatically.

Jeff was stunned. This was not what he was expecting. "Youuuu were?" he said. "I mean . . . I *know* you were. But *you* know you were?"

Over the next few minutes, I did my best to briefly explain to Jeff that I had been on a journey of *relearning* the gospel. I had come to realize that I needed to be evangelized all over again, not by the gospel of "you can avoid hell," but by the gospel of the Kingdom of Heaven—the gospel that Jesus preached and practiced.

Since the day I became a Christian, I had considered

myself an evangelical. But truth be told, I *wasn't*. Not in any biblical sense of the word. Sure, I was a prototypical American evangelical, but I was not practicing an evangelical lifestyle that Jesus would have recognized. I agreed with and preached according to the criteria by which most theologians and contemporary scholars defined evangelicalism, but that was merely a technicality.[†] From any practical or functional perspective, I was at best a pseudo-evangelical. I had bought into the deception that being an evangelical Christian meant I would vote for a certain political party and would get behind a set of ideologies and definitions that categorized people as "for God" or "against God" in correlation to their religious scruples and politics.

An authentic evangelical should be a "good news" person. And not just any old good news. This is about the good news of the Kingdom of Heaven—the good news that Jesus brought, lived, and taught. Somewhere along the line, I had lost track of the most important part of being evangelical. Over the years since then, I've found that I'm not alone.

Re-evangelizing Ourselves

Not long ago, I spoke at a conference for some wonderful pastors and leaders whose group name includes the word *evangelical*. Beginning the talk with a quick survey, I asked, "What does the term *evangelical* mean to you?" In response,

---

† Evangelical Christianity values the importance of the Bible as ultimate truth and authority, the need for conversion via a born-again experience of belief in Jesus Christ as the only way to eternal life, and the commissioning of all followers of Jesus to express and demonstrate the gospel through missionary activity and social reform.[3]

I heard a few scattered chuckles, but no one answered the question. They all just stared at me inquisitively, as if to say, "Huh? Everyone knows what that means."

Intrigued by this unanticipated stalemate, I smiled and pressed the point further. "Come on, you guys. You go by the name *evangelical*. What does the word mean when you trace it to its roots?"

With a bit of prodding, we were finally able to agree that the word *evangelical* comes from the same word as *gospel*

"Okay," I said, "what is the gospel?" Again, an awkward hush filled the auditorium. Only a bit of nervous seat-shifting could be heard. Finally, after some coaxing, a few folks began to call out familiar phrases such as, "To receive Jesus as your savior" and "To be assured of eternity in heaven." Someone even shouted, "John 3:16!"

"Is that it?" I asked. "Are you sure? That's all you've got? *That* is the gospel?"

This was as dedicated and sincere a group of ministers as you could hope to meet. They were men and women who had staked their careers and dedicated their lives for the sake of something very specific. They just weren't exactly sure what that specific something was. That was a telling moment.

Since that day, I have conducted the same experiment with dozens of similar groups, and the results are always the same. Each time, the scenario plays out like déjà vu. It's a sobering situation that we evangelicals must face head-on. Is it possible that we have somehow missed the crux of the gospel? Has our gospel gotten too small?

Having grown up in a conservative evangelical home, having married into a conservative evangelical family, and having pastored conservative evangelicals since I was nineteen, I'm fairly certain I would qualify for the Certified Evangelical seal of approval. I point this out to emphasize that I am writing from *inside* the camp. I haven't abandoned the tribe, nor do I intend or expect to. But I am convinced that we evangelicals—we bringers of good news—need to be *re*-evangelized. We need it for our own well-being, not to mention its necessity if we have any hope of reaching our neighbors and the broader world to which we've been sent. Before we evangelize anyone else, we need to re-evangelize ourselves.

On several occasions, I have heard my friend Mark Labberton, president of Fuller Theological Seminary, repeat a statement that his father often made: "Religion takes great things and makes them small." I'm afraid this statement applies to us as evangelicals, as well. We have reduced the gospel to a "plan of salvation" that has more to do with the afterlife than with our actual lives—our *right-here-right-now* lives. One of the most troubling aspects of this reduction of the gospel is that evangelicals have come to be seen as a people who care only about eternity, while not showing the same concern for people's lives—which calls into question how much we truly care about their eternal souls. The way we treat people here and now says we don't really care about their lives here and now. It reminds me of a story told by the great Methodist missionary and theologian E. Stanley Jones:

The evangelism of Jesus was an evangelism to the total man. He did not love people's souls alone—he loved people. A Hindu student came back from the West and said, "If those people had loved me a little bit more and my soul a little bit less, I might have become a Christian." Jesus did not go around loving people's souls—he loved people, and would lift everything that cramped body, soul, or mind.[4]

Sadly, for many evangelicals, the gospel has been shriveled and shrunken to the point that we have made the great Good News small. Like so many of my friends and family, I had come to believe and preach a gospel that focuses on our sinful separation from God, who wants to restore us to a right relationship with himself so that he won't have to destroy us with his unstinting holiness and we can be with him in heaven. That's certainly true, and it's an important part of the gospel message, but it's not the complete message. Focusing only on the "sin" question is like serving someone a plate of shelled pecans after promising a slice of pecan pie. The pecans are an essential part of the pie, but they are not the whole pie.

I came to realize that I needed to be truly "converted"— that is, genuinely and deeply changed—by the *entire* gospel, a gospel that goes well beyond mere mental assent to a list of propositional truths about Jesus that will save me from the ultimate consequences of my sinful nature and ensure that I go to heaven when I die. My understanding of the word *evangelical* needed to be restored to a more well-rounded and complete definition that includes belief in all the truth statements about Jesus, but also means committing to *live my life* according to Jesus' example in the most literal sense possible—as crazy as that may sound.

In the remainder of this book, I will explain the key points that have helped me in my continuing journey of reconversion to biblical evangelicalism, and I will share stories and examples of other Christians on this same journey, whom I have come to refer to as "revangelicals."

Revangelicals are followers of Jesus who have moved beyond merely favoring Jesus with their *belief* in him and have committed themselves to actually *following* him with the substance of their day-to-day lives. They take Jesus' words very personally, and often quite literally, and are convinced that his example is indeed a *livable* model and standard for us to emulate. Revangelicals are those who seek to live their lives as *Good News people* of the Kingdom of Heaven, even if it costs them the American Dream.

Revangelicals don't necessarily fit into political boxes. They refuse to let the Good News that Jesus proclaimed become co-opted and distilled by ideologies that conflict with the life and practice that Jesus taught and modeled. The gospel they believe in is too big and too awe-inspiring to fit perfectly into a political camp, platform, or agenda—whether liberal, conservative, Republican, Democrat, Independent, Tea Party, or whatever.

Revangelicals have come to the conclusion that if what

Jesus taught and commanded is too impractical for the real world, then the real world must be false. I have found in my own efforts to live out the principles in this book that my heart needs to be continually recalibrated to the Good News of the gospel of Jesus each and every day. My hope is that you can use the following pages to fine-tune your heart as well. May we all be *revangelicaled*.

QUESTIONS FOR REFLECTION

1. What is or has been your definition of the term *evangelical Christian*?
2. What is your definition of *the gospel*?
3. In what ways has your concept of the gospel opened or closed your life to others?
4. In what ways do you need a reconversion to the gospel of Jesus Christ?

2
REPENT

Martin Luther King gets to call himself a Christian because he actually practiced loving his enemies.

BILL MAHER

These days nearly two out of every five young outsiders (38 percent) claim to have a "bad impression of present-day Christianity." Beyond this, one-third of young outsiders said that Christianity represents a negative image with which they would not want to be associated.

DAVID KINNAMAN AND GABE LYONS, *UNCHRISTIAN*

You are the salt of the earth, but if salt has lost its taste, how shall its saltiness be restored? It is no longer good for anything except to be thrown out and trampled under people's feet.

MATTHEW 5:13

A WHILE BACK, I preached a sermon based on Matthew 5:13. Like many pastors, I had read or heard this verse hundreds, if not thousands, of times. But on this occasion something jumped off the pages of my Bible and seemed to hover in the air above my desk. Certain words stood out as if highlighted by one of those wide, yellow, felt-tip markers.

In particular, Jesus' words "If salt has lost its taste" caught my attention and got me thinking: *Can salt lose its taste? Have I ever tasted bad salt?*

I had never heard of such a thing. In all the cooking shows I had watched on television, I could not recall ever hearing a chef say, "Watch out for the bland salt." I began to wonder if it is even possible for salt to go bad. So I went online to try to answer the question. After a half hour of research, I went downstairs to confirm the findings with my wife.

Sherri is our in-house expert on all things having to do with food, cooking, gardening, and the like. I call her an *organic maven*. If she echoed what I had read in the web articles about salt, I would be convinced.

"Babe, I'm pretty sure I know the answer to this, but I need you to confirm. Is it possible for salt to expire or go bad?"

"Noooo," she replied, shaking her head and looking at me as if I had just asked her to confirm the existence of the Tooth Fairy.

Summoning me to the kitchen pantry, she pulled out a variety of salts from all over the world. (Like I said, she's our in-house expert.) The only salt that could lose its essence, as far as she knew, was Dead Sea salt, which is a mixture of minerals that could possibly be contaminated by foreign substances, causing the salt to become inedible.

Following a (very interesting) fifteen-minute lecture on the history and nuances of different varieties of salt, and the assurance that salt does not lose its flavor apart from being severely diluted or radically altered chemically, I was allowed to return to my sermon prep.

Scholars debate whether Jesus was speaking metaphorically about salt losing its savor, as an example of something that just doesn't happen, or if he was referring to the type of Dead Sea salt that could possibly become corrupted. Either way, bad salt is useless as a flavor enhancer. It has no good purpose. So Jesus' words are a warning to his followers throughout history: "You are the salt of the earth; but if you lose your saltiness, you will be considered as good for nothing, and people will trample whatever you do or say. They will dismiss you and your message as useless."

I'm convinced that this warning is especially timely for today's church in the West. But perhaps Jesus' words have become so familiar that we no longer hear the cautionary tone. Yet, current data—polls, research, books, and articles—reveal an alarming truth: Evangelical Christianity is in a rapidly trending decline, losing close to fifty thousand people per week. Much of the research points to increasingly off-putting views that non-Christians have about evangelicals. Not only do many non-Christians hold a negative opinion of evangelicals, but also a growing number of young Christians are leaving the ranks of evangelicalism for the same reasons. The research consistently shows that non-Christians view evangelicals as judgmental, unkind, demeaning, and the like, and that these negative perceptions are yielding a shrinking population of churchgoers.

The question we evangelicals must ask ourselves is this: How is it that the very people Jesus died to establish as models of forgiveness, gentleness, peace, and mercy have become a people generally perceived as mean, judgmental, and merciless? Right under our noses, the salt has lost its savor.

Before You Meet My Folks

I grew up in the progressive Dallas/Fort Worth suburbs, but my family spent about half our weekends with my grandparents about an hour north of Dallas. This meant I shared a lot of my childhood with uncles, aunts, and cousins who lived along gravel roads and farm fields. Just about all my relatives are from this region of North Texas, a place that is a bit frozen in time—not completely iced over, but still not quite thawed out.

My kinfolk are country folk. Some of them are *extremely* country. I'm talking reality-TV country. It seems that everyone up that way goes by his or her first *and* middle names. There are lots of Bettsie Maes, Bobby Joes, and Billy Rays. When I first heard Jeff Foxworthy tell his "You Might Be a Redneck If . . ." jokes, I thought he was describing my dad's side of the family.

When I was a teenager, a couple of my buddies and I would drive up north every so often to go camping or fishing in the area where my father grew up. But before I brought any of my friends around to meet my kinfolk, I tried to prepare them for the encounter. My relatives were good people, and I felt comfortable with them because they were *my* people. But they were quite different from the friends who made up the majority of my world, and the truth was, I was a bit embarrassed by them. I loved my family, but I wasn't too keen on having my day-to-day friends meet some of them.

As an evangelical Christian, I have to confess that I feel

the same way about many of the folks who make up my evangelical family. Though I've been a Christian for as long as I can remember, and I've been a pastor or church leader in one capacity or another since I was nineteen and have spent the last thirty years trying to promote Jesus and his church, I'm quite often embarrassed to admit I'm a Christian to people I've just met. It's not that I'm ashamed of Jesus, mind you. It's the rest of the family that troubles me. I love my evangelical kinfolk, but I'm not always eager to have my non-Christian friends meet some of them. In fact, I am finding it harder and harder to call myself an evangelical Christian. A while back, in looking for a new way to describe my beliefs, I began referring to myself as a "Goodnewsical Jesusian." But that was a bit clunky, so I settled on "revangelical."

The issue for evangelicals is not simply that Christian morals are often viewed as outdated in the culture at large. It's more that our eyes have become fixated on the surface issues of our fallen culture to such a degree that we have become convinced our only hope is to *fix* or *change* the system. Along the way, we have become known to the watching world more for what we are *against* than what we are *for*. We have become identified with political agendas, culture wars, and religious demands that leave non-Christians shaking their heads and dismissing Christianity altogether. We seem to have forgotten that Jesus didn't come to *fix* the system; he came to rescue us *from* the system and set our feet on a new, redemptive pathway. Jesus didn't come to overthrow the Roman Empire— the fallen cultural system of his day—though some of his disciples hoped and expected he would. He came to establish a *new* Kingdom, a radically subversive Kingdom, based on serving one another, healing divisions and diseases, and restoring loving relationships (between ourselves and other people, and ourselves and God).

I have come to dread the election season because of the vitriol that surfaces from many evangelicals. I'm not saying the bad blood doesn't come from non-Christians as well, but it *shouldn't* come from us evangelicals. People who have little Bible knowledge or Christian background are confounded by the non-Christlike attitudes of politically charged evangelicals. It pains me to say it, but too often I have to agree with the many comedians who riff on the disparity between what Jesus modeled and taught and the overarching persona of modern-day evangelical Christians. They say, "I don't go to church, but I'm pretty sure Jesus didn't treat people the way that so many Christians today treat people."

There's a better way for us to approach elections and the political process. Here are a few thoughts:

Commit to blessing. Refuse to curse. As the people who carry and speak the Good News of God's Kingdom, our mouths should be used to glorify God and to demonstrate that our first and ultimate trust is in him. Imagine how it would be if, during election seasons, the majority of Christians committed themselves to pray for God's conviction, wisdom, and truth to shine in and through our political candidates, while also refusing to speak vile and angry words about candidates with whom they disagreed.

First of all, then, I urge that supplications, prayers, intercessions, and thanksgivings be made for all people, for kings and all who are in high positions, that we may lead a peaceful and quiet life, godly and dignified in every way.

1 TIMOTHY 2:1-2

Be thankful for democracy. The freedom to elect our representatives is a privilege that people throughout history have died for, and that many are currently fighting for throughout the world. As tiring and frustrating as an election season can be, the process is the freedom fruit of democracy. Let gratitude prevail over grumbling during the voting season.

Refuse to be partisan. No movement or political party has cornered the market on the ways and means of the Lord. To pull the straight party lever in the ballot box, without objectively researching and studying the issues and candidates, is both irresponsible and short-sighted. Make every nominee earn your vote on the merits of his or her record and your dutifully researched understanding of how you believe that person will represent your God-shaped beliefs.

Put your trust in the Lord. Keep in mind that Jesus is the King of kings and Lord of lords. History is in his hands. It is *his* story. God is not wringing his hands as the networks report on the election returns. Do your due diligence, and share your viewpoints with others. Get involved in a candidate's campaign, if you feel so inclined. But regardless of how the election turns out, hand over the results to the Lord and trust his ultimate governance.

Maintain generous discourse. Both in your real life conversations or in cyberlife chatter, commit to maintaining a kind and thoughtful demeanor in what you say or post. When the peace of God rules our hearts, it is evident in the way we talk and type. Maintaining an open and teachable heart and mind is the only way to learn and grow. Seeking to understand the viewpoints of others allows us to learn from and be heard by them as well.

Keep in mind your true citizenship. As Christ followers, our heavenly citizenship (Philippians 3:20) trumps our earthly loyalties at every turn—including our patriotism and politics. Recently, I've had to unfollow the posts of many evangelical friends on Facebook because of their compassionless, shameless, even hateful comments as they take a stance for or against certain political candidates or issues. No doubt some of these brothers and sisters in Christ have unfollowed me as well because of my challenges to their posts. It saddens me that the very same people who frequently post Scripture verses and quotes declaring their love and allegiance to Jesus can at the same time exhibit such partisan bitterness, sarcasm, and contempt for others.

As Erwin Lutzer, pastor of the famous Moody Church in Chicago, writes:

Unfortunately, Christianity, in the minds of millions of Americans, is right-wing politics. I believe we are under judgment because we have cast about for a solution to our nation's problems and thought that it lay with political muscle and even with a specific political party. By becoming publicly partisan and implying that one party is more "Christian," we have clouded the issues of what Christianity really is. Religion is being redefined as politics; the flag has replaced the cross. And we are feeling the negative repercussions. Today evangelicals are in the news not because of the gospel but because of their political support or endorsements.[1]

It can be difficult to say anything about the intersection of faith and society without being categorized politically by any number of camps, and therefore dismissed with, "Oh, you're one of *them*." And that's frustrating. So let me make it clear that I'm not writing from a Republican or Democrat or Libertarian or Independent political perspective. I'm writing as one Christ follower to other Christ followers. This book is not intended to be a political book. But I understand that any exploration of the subject of evangelicalism in America will inevitably intersect with the issue of politics. Politics has become an identifier and definer to such a degree that the subject is unavoidable, even when one is straightforwardly trying to encourage evangelicals to *be* the *Good News people* that the label "evangelical" proclaims.

As a lifelong evangelical, I'm pleading with other evangelicals to take another look at where we're coming from. Let's stop for a minute and assess our philosophy. Does a gospel perspective shape our worldview? Are we not only preaching but also *practicing* the gospel that Jesus taught?

It is not my aim to sway people to vote for one party over another. I am far more concerned about our posture and disposition toward other people in our society and how we display the gospel and live it out. What is the point of casting a godly vote in the ballot box if all the while we're maintaining an ungodly attitude toward other people, one that does a great disservice to the cause of Christ?

The gospel of God's Kingdom—the gospel that Jesus brought us—is something incredibly beautiful when lived out in the lives of God's people. The apostle Paul writes, "I am not ashamed of the gospel of Christ."[2] Well, neither am I! I love the gospel of Jesus, not merely because it saves people from hell, but because it takes hell out of people right here and right now. I love the gospel because of the changed people it produces—people who live to give rather than to take, and who do for others as they would hope to have done to them. But I am extremely ashamed of the inferior, imposter gospel that has largely supplanted it in the hearts and actions of so many evangelicals.

When I first discussed this book with my publisher, I told them I would be writing from the perspective of a pastor. I worked as a pastor for more than two decades and that is my mind-set in approaching this topic. I have kept in touch with many members of the churches I served during my pastoral years, and they are some of the most wonderful people I have known in my life. But my heart often sinks when I see some of their comments and posts on social media that directly conflict with and contradict the Good News of Jesus' Kingdom. It reminds me of the account in the Gospel of Luke when the occupants of a certain Samaritan village rejected Jesus, and two of his disciples asked him if he wanted them to call down fire from heaven to consume the villagers. Jesus rebuked the disciples, saying, "You do not know what kind of spirit you are of."[3] When I hear or read the snarky comments and judgments of some evangelicals, I want to grab them by the shoulders and say, "This is not who we are! We have the spirit of Jesus in us. He created us to produce love, joy, peace, patience, kindness, goodness, faithfulness, gentleness, and self-control.[4] All this fear-laced, angry thinking and speaking is not from our Lord. C'mon, folks, we're better than this."

A New Operating System

A few years ago, one of my daughters became increasingly frustrated with a series of crashes and viruses on her PC laptop. Several family members had switched to Apple computers in the preceding year and my daughter desperately wanted a Mac. One evening, I looked across the living room and saw her typing away on what appeared to be an Apple laptop. I grabbed my glasses and looked closer. Turned out she didn't have a new Mac; she had simply taken an Apple logo sticker and placed it over the brand logo on her PC. I laughed and said, "Hey, how's that working out for you?"

Placing an Apple sticker on her PC accomplished nothing other than to cause others to think, at first glance, that she had switched to a Mac. The problem for her was that the operating system hadn't changed.

Following Jesus means to actually *follow him*. We don't just get a new label; we change our entire operating system. Essentially, it means we get a new point of view—on everything. We don't simply give mental assent to an intellectual belief in Jesus' existence, or even just confess with our mouths that he is the Son of God. Following Jesus means we seek to live our lives as if it were *Jesus* living our lives. That is the game changer in discipleship. That is the operating system conversion.

To be a disciple—a true follower—of Jesus doesn't mean we merely *like* Jesus, like a thumbs-up on his Facebook page. It means we choose to *be like* Jesus. There is a lot to like about Jesus, not the least of which is the truth that believing in him yields eternal salvation. But one of the problems with contemporary Christianity is that we have made eternal salvation the end product, when all the while it is but a by-product of surrendering our lives to Jesus. (We will discuss this in greater depth later in the book.)

The journey of following Jesus and becoming more and more like him is a *progression*. It is something we will not fully attain in this life; but by committing ourselves to be *continually changed* by Jesus, we gradually and persistently become more like him. The key to our progress is believing that Jesus is *right* about everything and therefore surrendering our own will to his. The constant hurdle we face is that his point of view, which is one and the same with the perspective of God's Kingdom, is often contrary to our worldly kingdom point of view. Moreover, the ways and means of God's Kingdom are most often counterintuitive to our ways and means and in conflict with our human reasoning.

Let's face it: Jesus is full of *non*sense. The apostle Paul calls it the "folly" of the cross.[5] It doesn't make sense, for instance, to turn the other cheek. It doesn't make sense to love our enemies. It doesn't make sense to bless those who curse us. It doesn't make sense to do good to those who hate us.[6] A lot of what Jesus says just *doesn't make sense.* But placing our faith in Jesus means that we trust him even when what he says to do (or how he tells us to respond) doesn't jibe with what our rational minds tell us to do. Part of what it means to *believe in him* is that we continue to move forward in *obedience to him* even if we don't fully understand or agree with his approach.

Recall the father who brought his son to Jesus to be healed of an unclean spirit. Jesus said to the man, "All things are possible for one who believes."[7] The father replied, "I believe; help my unbelief!"[8] That was good enough for Jesus. He healed the boy. I'm convinced that this father was telling Jesus that he believed in him personally, but was still struggling with the circumstances that were in front of his eyes.

As we grow in our experience of placing our trust (faith) in Jesus in the course of our day-to-day lives, we will see him show up in amazing ways. And as we continue this journey of faith, our capacity for trusting Jesus will grow to the extent that we will find ourselves less and less often needing to pray, "Lord, help my unbelief." This is what the process of being transformed into citizens of God's Kingdom looks like. *Our point of view inexorably changes.* We begin to see all of life from a *Kingdom* perspective rather than from a Republican, Democrat, or American point of view.

The Bible clearly teaches that placing our trust in the systems of the world—like building with wood, hay, and straw—will not survive the purifying fire of the Kingdom of God.[9] The earthly systems on which we have built our lives will be burned up in the furnace of faith. That's why the gospel of the Kingdom is a threat to every power that is not of itself. Jesus made it clear that the new wine of God's Kingdom cannot be stored in the old wineskins of our earthly ways and means.[10]

Why *They* Like Jesus

When reading the Gospels, have you ever noticed that it's always the religious folks who are running Jesus out of their churches (synagogues) and towns? And it's always the people on the margins—the outcasts, the untouchables, the lower classes—who flock to Jesus like sheep in need of a shepherd. When Jesus says, "Blessed are the poor in spirit" (Matthew 5:3), he's not talking about people who are just going through a little rough patch in life. The term he uses refers to people at the bottom of the heap, the most despised *nobodies*. Jesus speaks to the very ones whom society—including all the religious folks—have called worthless and useless, and says, "I am *for* you! I value you richly. My agenda has you front and center."

Jesus was far too inclusive for the comfort of the religious leaders and church folk of his day. He constantly cut holes in the legal fences erected by the Pharisees, broke off the chains barring the ceremonial gates, and cracked the code to the doors of the Temple. His inclusion of women in his inner circle, his eating and drinking with tax collectors, and the parable he told about a *Good* Samaritan were more than the religious establishment could bear. That parable alone was beyond outrageous. Perhaps the best way for us to understand the scandal of Jesus' teaching about the Good Samaritan would be to recast the story in contemporary terms as "the parable of the good Muslim." I think that would be an accurate parallel.

Please don't misunderstand. I'm not saying there are no good Muslims, any more than Jesus was saying there were no good Samaritans. In fact, that's precisely the point.

In the eyes of the Pharisees, Jesus committed treason against every notable institution of his day—family, religion, and nationalism. He redefined each one and reordered our allegiances. Then, to top it off, he went after the "golden goose" of resources and materialism. This hits us evangelicals—us "gospel people"—right in the breadbasket. For if *our* gospel is not first and foremost a gospel to the same poor that Jesus addressed in his gospel, then we have a different gospel altogether. The gospel of the Kingdom of God challenges, demands, upsets, and overtakes everything we have built from any source that is contrary to God.

If We Were Jesus

No doubt you've heard some version of the saying, "God created man in his own image and then man returned the favor."[11] It serves as a good reminder that we must continually evaluate our *image* of Jesus against our own worldviews, attitudes, and actions. In other words, if we can't find evidence in Scripture that Jesus had the same attitudes we have toward other people, then we had better check our sources. Where did we get this mind-set? What is our attitude toward the poor? Do we view the needy in America as lazy folks who have not taken advantage of their opportunities? Do we view terrorists with a hatred that makes us happy when they die, or at the very least, do we flippantly shrug our shoulders when they are killed or tortured? If we were sitting on the couch with Jesus, watching the evening news, and a story came on about a terrorist getting blown up, is there anything in the way Jesus interacted with people in the Bible to suggest he would respond by saying, "Ha! Too bad. But that guy had it coming"? Would Jesus cheer at what we cheer for, or would he weep?

What are some issues that Jesus would be most vocal about or take a noteworthy stand on? Would he spend the same amount of energy on the political causes we spend our mental, vocal, and actionable energy on? Or would he spend it in other ways?

We see in the Gospels that it's the outsiders—the lame, the poor, the blind, the prostitutes, the drunkards, the tax collectors, the sinners, and the foreigners—who tend to follow Jesus. It is those on the inside and at the top who crucify him: the elders, chief priests, teachers of the Law, and Roman occupiers. Doesn't that tell us something important about our *perspective*?

Every perspective is a view from a particular vantage point. Before the apostle Paul's conversion, he was certain he was against what God was against. But Jesus confronted him and asked, "Why are you persecuting me?"[12] Paul was blind for several days after this encounter, signifying that his way of seeing was, in effect, darkness and spiritual blindness. If we want to see the truth, we must continually critique our own perspectives and positions in light of what Jesus taught and modeled. Are we for and against the same things that Jesus was for and against?

The Bible says we have the mind of Christ (1 Corinthians 2:16), but we need his *eyesight*, as well. Too many evangelicals read the Bible from the perspective of the powerful and privileged, the comfortable and secure. But Jesus consistently taught from the viewpoint of the poor and the oppressed. That's why he said, "It is not the healthy who need a doctor, but the sick" (Mark 2:17, NIV).

While protecting our "rights" and privileges as citizens in the "kingdom of America," we have largely lost sight of the truth of the Kingdom of God and the demands it makes on us. Therefore, we tend to chase after things that Jesus either never chased after or flat-out told us to turn from. We can do better. We *must* do better.

An Untweetable Gospel

I've come to realize that many, if not most, evangelicals became Christians by buying into a "tweeted" version of the gospel.

> Jesus died for my sins and gave me eternal life. God said it, I believe it, that settles it. Heaven's gonna be awesome. #boundforglory

> Made a decision for Christ & have a personal relationship with Jesus. Saved from the devil & the fires of hell. #Iam4given #john316

For many of us, it seemed to work. The gospel is so powerful that even a portion of it is strong enough to change someone's life. But for others, their "decision for Jesus" failed to truly *convert* them to the pursuit of a Christlike life. It is estimated that as many as 50 percent of those who make "decisions for Christ" do not actually give their lives to following Jesus.[13] In other words, they do not become *disciples*.

Twitter is a wonderful tool. But it's a double-edged sword. Its very strength is also its greatest weakness. Because tweets are limited to no more than 140 characters, including punctuation and spaces, every message must be reduced to its barest essentials. There are even "tweet shrink" websites to help make messages short enough to post.

But while brevity is the soul of wit (Shakespeare would have knocked 'em dead on Twitter), it's not always the best way to communicate. In Twitter's brief history, countless celebrities, athletes, politicians, and Christian leaders have had to explain their way out of fixes they got themselves into when those 140 characters failed to deliver the intended message. Tweets often communicate an incomplete, muted, or twisted version of the author's message because certain ideas, opinions, or stories are impossible—or at least difficult—to convey in such limited terms.

The same is true of our evangelism. If we start with a truncated gospel and simply retweet it, the gospel we pass along may not be a false gospel, but it is certainly a *reduced* or *incomplete* gospel.

This scaled-down gospel has had an effect on the way we see others, as well. Actually, I should say that our minimized gospel has *failed* to affect the way we see others, beyond a casual concern for their afterlife. I mean, who wants to see someone go to hell? But it's hard for people to believe we care about the possibility of their spending eternity in hell if we don't seem to care that they are living in hell on earth right now.

In many ways, our "personal relationship with Jesus" has fed a passive disregard for others. We were taught that the bottom line of the gospel is the issue of heaven and hell. Who's in and who's out. That always seems to be the *big question*. But is that really the gospel? Is that the message Jesus brought?

The issue of heaven or hell is *included* in the gospel. Absolutely. The name *Jesus* means "Yahweh is salvation." But the gospel doesn't begin and end with questions about the afterlife. Jesus brings redemption and salvation for the *whole* of our lives—including the part we're living *right now*, and including all of creation. Though the issue of our eternal destiny is included in the gospel, it's impossible to read the New Testament and come away with a tweet-sized message that centers on issues of heaven or hell.

And though it's also true that Jesus died on the cross to pay for our sins, in all my reading of the four Gospels, the book of Acts, and the Epistles, I cannot come up with anything remotely close to the "sinner's prayer" as an entry point to the Kingdom of Heaven.

That statement may be quasi-heretical to some of my evangelical brothers and sisters. We have grown up with the sinner's prayer. It has been our silver bullet. Most likely, we prayed it ourselves. But I don't find Jesus using it or teaching it. Nor do any of the apostles or other New Testament evangelists.

So if the gospel isn't as simple as praying the sinner's prayer or making a decision for Christ, what is it? What are we missing?

For starters, the gospel *is* good news, but it's not good news about *us* and our final destination. It's not good news about how we will enter heaven after we die. It's good news about God's in-breaking Kingdom. The good news is that God invites us to enter the Kingdom of Heaven right now!

Many people think of Jesus as our Savior, as the one who will get us into heaven. So the question often is "Have I accepted Jesus as my Savior?" But we never ask the question "Have I accepted Jesus as my teacher?" And that's the real question. With the disciples, it began there. They began by accepting him as their teacher, and then accepting him as their Savior—which included, of course, their eternal destiny—was a natural outflow of that. But they started with Jesus as their teacher, because we all have to learn how to live.[14]

We are invited into the ethics and economy of God's Kingdom, his reign and his rule, his idea of how society should operate. The gospel is the Good News of this Kingdom ethic—the "on earth as it is in heaven" that Jesus instructed his disciples to pray for and seek after.[15] (As we move forward in the book, we will go deeper into what this looks like in our actual lives.)

The Gospel according to Jesus

Soon after his encounter with Satan in the wilderness (Matthew 4:1-11), Jesus made his way to the synagogue in his hometown of Nazareth to publicly announce his ministry. Scholars often refer to this as his kingly inaugural speech. It is here that Jesus defines the gospel . . . his gospel of the Kingdom. This was going to be good news indeed. This would be the best news the world had ever heard.

And the scroll of the prophet Isaiah was given to him. He unrolled the scroll and found the place where it was written,

"The Spirit of the Lord is upon me,
   because he has anointed me
   to proclaim good news to the poor.
He has sent me to proclaim liberty to the captives
   and recovering of sight to the blind,
   to set at liberty those who are oppressed,
to proclaim the year of the Lord's favor."

LUKE 4:17-19

This is our first overview of the gospel. We get it straight from the lips of Jesus. It has five clear and distinct aspects. Any expression of the gospel that lacks one or more of these components is not complete. And as Christians, if we don't understand and embrace these components, we need to be re-evangelized . . . re-*gospeled*.

Jesus calls his gospel "good news to the poor." It is good news for *those suffering economic defeat.*

He proclaims "liberty to the captives"—that is, freedom for *those held captive to social and political systems and power structures.*

He announces "recovering of sight to the blind." Throughout his earthly ministry, we see Jesus restore vision both to the *physically blind* and the *spiritually blind*.

He is sent by the Father to set free the *morally and spiritually bruised and oppressed.*

He proclaims "the year of the Lord's favor," a reference to the Jewish custom of Jubilee, which means a *new beginning* for those who were enslaved and a *restoring of inheritance* for those who had lost what was once rightfully theirs.[16]

This was the beginning of the good work that Jesus later commissioned his disciples to carry on.

> And *this gospel of the kingdom* will be proclaimed throughout the whole world as a testimony to all nations, and then the end will come.
> MATTHEW 24:14 (italics added)

Try It . . . You'll Like It

One thing I like about shopping at Sam's Club or Costco is sampling the food at stations scattered throughout the store, where shoppers are invited to try new foods and beverages. The product manufacturers believe that if people get even a taste of their product, they will like it and buy it.

That's how the church should be in the world—offering a delicious taste of the Kingdom of God so that people can see that the Lord is good (Psalm 34:8). The gospel is Good News precisely because it restores our right relationship with God and sets us free to be a part of the family of God. Moreover, it brings us into "the family business," proclaiming healing and freedom to all who will hear. When the gospel of the Kingdom of Heaven is alive and thriving in the hearts of

God's people, we get a foretaste of heaven on earth. Clenched fists become open hands that give care and healing; hardened hearts become softened. Our very lives become "sampling stations" of God's grace and mercy and goodness. That's what *evangelical Christian* should mean in our society—that we are people who bring the Good News of the Kingdom of Heaven to the places where we live, work, and play. Our lives and our words should bear witness to the truth that, in Jesus, all will be restored and everyone will be set free.

Jesus proclaims good news to the poor, not because the gospel is a prosperity pill, as falsely claimed by too many preachers, but because it is a prescription through which everyone's needs will be met.

Some preachers have tried to interpret "good news to the poor" as referring to the "spiritually poor." This *spiritualization* is often the first step in an attempt to escape the plain implications of the Word of God. If we take what Jesus says *literally*, it places a demand on our lives right now. But if we proclaim good news to the "spiritually poor," it poses no threat to our comfortable lifestyle. Spiritual poverty is an intangible need. But if Jesus meant *real* poor people, that's a different story and much harder to overlook. For if I encounter an actual poor person and my wallet's not empty, the demand to deliver on the Good News falls on me.

When Jesus tells his followers, "Do to others as you would have them do to you" (Luke 6:31, NIV), that should be good news to any poor people who encounter his followers. But if we spiritualize the "good news to the poor" and make it some sort of nebulous blessing to be enjoyed in eternity, what kind of good news is that? The good news that Jesus talked about shines through in his feeding of the multitudes on more than one occasion. He did not just want to satisfy their hunger, he also wanted to bring them together in life-giving relationships that would connect them to one another.

Something special happens when people sit down and break bread with one another. They tell their life stories, talk about their present situations—their hopes, dreams, fears, and joys—all while they are sharing a meal and time together. Just imagine hearing Jesus teach about how we should treat the *one anothers* around our tables and in our lives.

Turn Around

When John the Baptist began evangelizing, he called the people to *repentance*. (Now there's a word we don't use much these days!) For some, the word is rather harsh sounding, stirring up visions of street-corner preachers, sawdust-floor tent revivals, pithy bumper stickers, and ominous "gospel" tracts. But *repent* is not a complicated word; it simply means to turn around, to change direction. We see John's message of repentance in Luke's Gospel:

> [John] went into all the region around the Jordan,
> proclaiming a baptism of repentance for the
> forgiveness of sins. As it is written in the book of the
> words of Isaiah the prophet,

"The voice of one crying in the wilderness:
'Prepare the way of the Lord,
    make his paths straight.
Every valley shall be filled,
    and every mountain and hill shall be made low,
and the crooked shall become straight,
    and the rough places shall become level ways,
and all flesh shall see the salvation of God.'"

LUKE 3:3-6

He said therefore to the crowds that came out to be baptized by him, . . . "Bear fruits in keeping with repentance."

LUKE 3:7-8

And the crowds asked him, "What then shall we do?" And he answered them, "Whoever has two tunics is to share with him who has none, and whoever has food is to do likewise."

LUKE 3:10-11

Notice that John did not allow the crowds to define repentance as mere *mental assent* to the ideas he proclaimed. He demanded *fruit* that aligned with their proclaimed repentance. In other words, "If you change your mind, you'll also change your life."

John preached a gospel designed to straighten out a crooked world. It was a revolutionary message aimed to bring down those on the mountaintop and bring up those living in the valleys of despair. This was good news to the poor, the socially and politically disenfranchised, and those living under the guilt and shame of their own self-induced sin and immorality. This gospel of repentance has implications on earth as well as for heaven. Repentance means not only turning away from our individual sins, but also turning away from the greedy, get-everything-you-can world system.

The gospel of the in-breaking Kingdom of Heaven is good news to the poor because it changes the prevailing *culture*. It breaks down walls of disparity between the *haves* and the *have-nots*. When we preach an abbreviated gospel that is primarily about salvation from hellfire after we die, nothing comes from it to change the culture here and now. It falls short of "your kingdom come, your will be done, on earth as it is in heaven" (Matthew 6:10). Jesus intended for his gospel to noticeably affect society and the way people treat one another. When the gospel takes hold of people's hearts and minds, they begin to embody the essence of "on earth as in heaven." Our efforts are never perfect, and we cannot fully alleviate, or escape, the effects of this broken world. But our basic *pursuits* and *priorities* change. And as we approach life differently, our lives become appealing and attractive to a watching world.

Sherilyn "Sher" Sheets is one revangelical whose priorities and pursuits changed when she and her faith community began to reevaluate their ideas and definitions of evangelism in light of their claims to be followers of Jesus. These conversations spurred Sher's conviction that the poor and homeless need *friends* just as much as they need food. So she began eating at the same soup kitchen where she volunteered in the Uptown neighborhood of Chicago.

"We didn't want to just come in with our guitars and Bible studies," she says. "We wanted to build relationships among the homeless community in our neighborhood."

Before long, she had created a role for herself at a neighborhood homeless shelter. She told the managers that she felt called to be *with* the clients as they came to receive the shelter's services. She started by playing cards with folks as they waited their turn. As she got to know the people on a personal level, she gained a greater understanding of their needs.

One day, it occurred to her that many of her homeless friends deserved to have a birthday party. So she started hosting a monthly party for anyone born in that particular month, complete with decorations, ice cream, and cupcakes. Sher refuses to serve store-bought cupcakes. "They have to be homemade," she says. "I don't want us to just buy something to give to them. We must put our hearts and time into it."

In addition to the birthday parties, her community ministry, called JUSTembrace, hosts monthly foot clinics, where Sher and her fellow revangelicals wash the feet of the homeless in warm footbaths, followed by foot massages and the clipping of toenails. Sher says, "If your mother or grandmother could not take care of her feet, you would do something about it. Those very people are our neighbors. That's why we do it."[17]

But Sher doesn't just *visit* the Uptown neighborhood. She lives there, along with a group of others who have joined her in what used to be a notorious drug house. They've chosen to live there for the sake of bringing restoration to broken lives through hospitality—a gospel edict through and through. Just a few years ago, people on Sher's street lived in fear and isolation; but in a relatively short period of time, a commitment to inclusivity and generosity has brought a deep sense of community and belonging. Lives are being changed by these Good News people.

The cultural implications of the gospel of the Kingdom are revolutionary. When the people asked John the Baptist what he meant by "bear fruits in keeping with repentance," he told them to share their surplus with the less fortunate, to not take more than their share, and to be content with what they have (Luke 3:8, 10-14). When Jesus came along, he taught us to care for "the least of these" (Matthew 25:40). In fact, he said that caring for the less fortunate was the same as caring for him (Matthew 25:34-40). That sheds some new light on the meaning of a "personal relationship with Jesus." When we try to spiritualize so much of what Jesus said, it removes the revolutionary sauce from the gospel.

The apostle Paul calls the gospel "the power of God for salvation" (Romans 1:16). But when the heart of the gospel message is reduced to "Good News" about what will happen to us after we die, it loses its power to change and reorient the direction of our lives and the lives of the people around us.

But when we invite people to join us in *following Jesus*,

it's a different matter altogether. Maybe it's time to replace the "sinner's prayer" with a "*follower's* prayer" that takes our repentance to its natural conclusion—not merely *turning around*, but also *moving in the right direction*—which is to say, building our lives on Jesus. He is, after all, "the way, and the truth, and the life" (John 14:6).

Similar to the sinner's prayer, in the follower's prayer we would admit culpability. We would admit our guilt against God and also admit that we have most often sinned against God by sinning against others. We would confess that we have hurt God most often by hurting others. We would admit that we have lived for ourselves, but by praying this prayer we express our repentance and our desire to do to others as we would have them do to us.

A return to the Good News of the gospel of Jesus will create a people who are known more for what they are *for* than for what they are against. If we are going to call ourselves evangelicals, we must *become* Good News people by allowing the Good News of the gospel to seep into our most deeply held assumptions and treasured ideologies. The gospel must shape our day in, day out approach to people and possessions. This means we embrace the foolishness of Jesus and his nonsensical ways and means. Revangelicals are people who refuse to accept a shrunken gospel, and who *press in* to the heart of Jesus to adopt and demonstrate his attitudes and actions toward others. Revangelicals embrace the things that Jesus embraces and put away the things he scorns.

Revangelicals are those Christians who seek to live their lives as Jesus would live if he were us.

QUESTIONS FOR REFLECTION

1. Consider the perception that many non-Christians have of evangelicals. In what ways have you dismissed or tried to understand such viewpoints?

2. Has your personal definition of the gospel reflected Jesus' definition, or have you embraced a reduced form of the gospel? How can you tell?

3. In what ways is your daily life a taste of the Kingdom of Heaven here on earth?

4. In your current response to embracing the Kingdom of Heaven, what "fruit of repentance" are you currently holding back?

3
RECOMMIT

*Jesus started preaching . . . "Change your life.
God's kingdom is here."*
MATTHEW 4:17, MSG

Jesus answered, "My kingdom is not of this world."
JOHN 18:36

ABOUT A YEAR after graduating from high school, I had an encounter with a stranger that changed the course of my life. She was a middle-aged lady who came to visit my parents on an evening when I was home to wash my clothes and enjoy some of my mom's homemade coconut pie. For several months, I had been living with a couple of buddies, all of us up to no good, in our own apartment across town. We all worked for the same landscaping company and lived for the weekends.

It was the early 1980s, and my plan was to make my way to a big city and live the dream of becoming a motorcycle cop. It wasn't necessarily that I was passionate about law enforcement, but one of my favorite television shows at the time was *CHiPs* (I realize that's like saying my favorite band was the Bee Gees), whose main characters were handsome young cops who patrolled the California freeways.

What was not to love about that life? You got to ride a motorcycle all day long and go to disco clubs and hang out with beautiful girls at night.

Back then, I was too young and foolish to realize that, with the direction my life was headed, I was more likely to wind up living in a van down by the river than cruising through LA on a KZ1000P. I had stepped away from my Christian upbringing and had no intention of coming back.

That all changed in a matter of minutes.

The woman who was visiting that evening was a *prayer warrior*—an intercessor who spent several hours each day in prayer. She had started her day at her home near Los Angeles, and after responding to a series of promptings through prayer, had ended up at my parents' house near Fort Worth. She was a friend of my parents' closest friends.

All evening, I made a point of staying near the baseball game on the television in the den, steering clear of the older folks in the dining room. But at one point, the woman came into the den and watched the game with me for a while, engaging me in baseball conversation. At the end of the evening, just before she left the house, she asked if it would be okay if she prayed for me.

I felt trapped. How do you tell someone that you don't want them to pray for you? So I yielded to her request.

That was more than thirty years ago and yet the evening remains indelibly vivid in my mind. As she began to pray, I kept one eye open, looking over her shoulder at the TV. But then it hit me. I can only describe it as what it might feel like to be dropped into a vat of liquid love. I was the Prodigal Son enveloped in the arms of the heavenly Father. After years of my essentially abandoning any attempt to follow Jesus, he now came running to me and bear-hugged me. Within a few days, I had moved back home, and over the next few months I immersed myself in the church my parents attended.

As grateful as I am for those early days of my life with Jesus, there's another part of the story that I never realized or considered until about ten years ago: *When I came back to the Lord, I left all my friends behind.* It was as if I stepped out of one world and into another, closing the door behind me. It wasn't that my friends turned away from me, but I, in effect, walked out of their lives.

Within a few short months, I began to view the world differently. A lot of that was very good. It was part of the transformation of my life to clean up my act and begin to think from a Jesus perspective. But along with the positive changes, a not-so-subtle "us vs. them" mentality crept in.

Based on the teaching I received at church, I began to label and sort people into categories. Saints and sinners. Holy and heathen. Godly and ungodly. Righteous and reprobate. In fact, the entire world was divided into two camps—the secular and the sacred—and it was clear who the "enemies of the gospel" were. Bible studies, small group meetings, and

church services now consumed the majority of my free time. These gatherings were viewed as a refuge from "the world," as my Christian friends and I called it.

In the culture at large, this was the peak season of the Moral Majority and the rise of the Christian Right. The three legs of the conservative platform focused on prayer in public schools, abortion, and the so-called gay agenda. I quickly got on board. Along with the vast majority of my evangelical contemporaries, I signed on for the mission of "taking America back for God" and "standing for what is right."

The two people groups that began to draw the greatest ire—pro-abortion advocates and homosexuals—became "enemies" in my eyes. Of course, if you had asked me, I would have said that I loved them. The problem was that my *professed* love had no tangible demonstration. It was love *in principle* (because the Bible commanded us to love), but it had no substantive manifestation. I had little chance to actually *show* love because I had no genuine relationships with anyone outside the camp. I didn't have any gay friends or close acquaintances. I didn't know anyone who was dealing with an unwanted pregnancy. And every one of my friends was just like me.

Today, I don't consider people who have differing viewpoints or differing lifestyles to be my enemies, but for the sake of illustration, let's say they *were* my enemies. Then what? I was never taught, in the churches of which I was a part, to treat those so-called enemies the way Jesus told us to treat our enemies—by *blessing* them. Those in my evangelical community and I were more likely to speak ill of people on

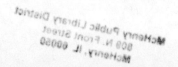

the "wrong side" of the political and moral aisle than we were to be gentle or genuinely kind. How quickly I forgot that I, too, had once been an enemy of God. Dallas Willard, the late scholar and Christian sage, speaks to this idea:

> Christians are routinely taught by example and word that it is more important to be right . . . than it is to be Christlike. In fact, being right licenses you to be mean, and, indeed, *requires* you to be mean— righteously mean, of course. . . .
>
> A fundamental mistake of the conservative side of the American church today, and much of the Western church, is that it . . . aims to get people into heaven rather than to get heaven into people. . . .
>
> [This] creates groups of people who may be ready to die, but clearly are not ready to live. They rarely can get along with one another, much less those "outside." Often their most intimate relations are tangles of reciprocal harm, coldness, and resentment. They have found ways of being "Christian" without being Christlike.[1]

The Empire Strikes Out

Growing up during the 1960s and '70s in what is often referred to as the Bible Belt, I was a firsthand observer as the church enjoyed its last days of having a "home field advantage." Back then, Christianity cast a long shadow across American society. Nativity scenes shone on courthouse lawns, the Ten Commandments hung in public school classrooms, and very few stores were open on Sundays. But the times they were a-changin' and church leaders soon found themselves spinning out, in want of traction on what had once been firm footing in the surrounding culture.

Since the fourth century, when Emperor Constantine converted to Christianity and declared it the official religion of the Roman Empire, Christians have enjoyed tremendous power and influence in the Western world. Constantine not only elevated the status of the church, he also lavished it with resources, protection, and favor. The impact of Constantine's conversion is hard to overstate. Here are some of the changes that occurred as a result:

- All citizens of the empire were assumed to be Christian by birth.
- A "sacral society" emerged, in which there was no effective distinction between religion and politics.
- Infant baptism became a symbol of incorporation into the Christian society.
- A supposedly Christian morality was imposed on the entire population (though mostly it meant the application of Old Testament moral standards).
- Sunday became a day of required church attendance, with penalties for noncompliance.
- The definition of *orthodoxy* as the common belief shared by all was determined by powerful church leaders supported by the state.

- Massive and ornate church buildings were erected.
- A strong distinction was drawn between clergy and laity, with the laity relegated to a largely passive role.
- The wealth of the church increased and citizens were obliged to tithe to fund the system.
- The world was divided between Christendom and heathendom, and wars were waged in the name of Christ and the church.
- Political and military force were used to impose the Christian faith.[2]

The rise of Christendom changed the character and focus of Christianity, which went from being "a dynamic, revolutionary, social, and spiritual movement to being a static religious institution" defined by its rituals, clergy, and buildings.[3] The Christian faith mutated from a vibrant way of life lived out 24/7 to an obligation fulfilled by a brief, weekly visit to a particular location.

In the United States, the underlying assumption has long been that Christianity is the predominant influencer of culture—or should be. We see this in the notion of America as a Christian nation. When the Bible is widely accepted as the undisputed Word of God, it can be used to settle arguments and set policy. But in a post-Christendom world, the Bible holds little or no authority among the majority. It might be acceptable and useful in the practice of one's private faith, but woe to the one who tries to bring it into the public square.

Europe saw the decline of Christendom in the middle of

the twentieth century, and America has quickly followed in her footsteps. The church has lost its position of prominence and influence. It is rapidly returning to its pre-Constantinian minority status. It's as if the church has come full circle. I've often heard author Reggie McNeal say, "It's AD 30 all over again" in the church today.

Certainly the days of Christian ascendency are over in America. Christians no longer set the agenda for American culture. Stores are routinely open on Sundays (in fact, it's more unusual if they're closed), and Wednesday evenings—the traditional night for midweek church services in the South—are no longer off limits to sporting events and other activities. Pregame prayers beneath the Friday night lights at the high school football field are a thing of the past. Christians who get upset by a department store's greeting of "Happy Holidays" rather than "Merry Christmas" are selling tickets for a ship that has already set sail. We have long since lost our favorite-son status.

The decline and fall of Christendom has left millions of Christians in a quandary. Many evangelicals are struggling to redefine their purpose and identity. Some have taken a defensive stance against the prevailing culture. Others have retreated into Christian subcultures to protect their families from the encroaching worldly system. Still others have left the church—in its traditional, institutional forms—frustrated that so many Christians haven't recognized that the party's over.

Reflecting on the decline of Christian influence in

America, many people look to the metaphor of *exile* as a descriptor of the new state of affairs. For many Christians, it is somewhat comforting to relate to the people of Israel, who were taken into Babylonian captivity in 586 BC. Many parallels can certainly be drawn. Displacement, uncertainty, marginalization, and an overall loss of identity all come with being exiled. But *exile* also evokes a desire and goal to be restored to a previous status and way of life—and I'm convinced that the gospel of the Kingdom of Heaven does not call us to such a hope. Many Christians seem to believe it is their duty to regain the hill of Christendom and rehoist the Christian flag. But I believe such efforts are misguided.

Though many Christians may feel frustrated, fearful, and out of sorts in the emerging twenty-first-century culture, our calling is not to go back to the good old days, whatever those might have been. God has not called us to old systems of moral superiority and political dominance; instead, he invites us into his Kingdom and to something altogether different—*renewal*.

As Christ followers, we are better served to look to the words of Jeremiah the prophet, who spoke for God during the time of the Jewish exile in Babylon:

Thus says the LORD of hosts, the God of Israel, to all the exiles whom I have sent into exile from Jerusalem to Babylon: Build houses and live in them; plant gardens and eat their produce. Take wives and have sons and daughters; take wives for

your sons, and give your daughters in marriage, that
they may bear sons and daughters; multiply there,
and do not decrease. But seek the welfare of the city
where I have sent you into exile, and pray to the
LORD on its behalf, for in its welfare you will find
your welfare.

JEREMIAH 29:4-7

Jeremiah challenged his Jewish brothers and sisters to resist
the desire to return and restore the empire of Israel. And he
encouraged them instead to accept their new situation as
God's will and to seek God's blessing on those they considered their enemies.

Many evangelicals today are like the Japanese soldiers in
the jungles and caves of Guam and Morotai who became
known as "holdouts" after the end of World War II. These
soldiers were either unaware that Japan had surrendered in
August 1945, or they simply refused to believe it. Even as
late as 1974, when Japan was well on its way to recovering
from the war and repositioning itself as an American ally
and financial superpower, at least one soldier still had not
surrendered.

In the American evangelical community today, more than
a few "soldiers of the Lord" are still holding out hope and
continuing to fight as if our "Christian nation" were still
intact. The marginalization of the church has caused tremendous anxiety for many of these people. They have responded
by focusing their energies on defending the last bastions of

Christian America, such as the definition of marriage. They continue to perceive the surrounding culture as an enemy to be resisted and defended against.

During my younger days, I often joined with the conservative Christian chorus that manifested itself in the "righteous meanness" that Dallas Willard spoke of. Along with my church leaders and friends, I thought nothing of verbally tearing down non-Christians (though not to their faces), telling and laughing at jokes about liberal politicians, and becoming apocalyptic in tone when discussing the fight against liberalism in our society. Like many of my fellow evangelicals, I ignored the clear New Testament teaching that strictly forbids mean and derisive speech against others. Consider the following verses, in light of a typical day's worth of social media posts and memes by evangelical Christians:

> "I'm sorry, brothers. I didn't realize he was the high priest," Paul replied, "for the Scriptures say, 'You must not speak evil of any of your rulers.'"
>
> ACTS 23:5, NLT

> Let all bitterness and wrath and anger and clamor and slander be put away from you, along with all malice.
>
> EPHESIANS 4:31

> Remind the believers to submit to the government and its officers. They should be obedient, always

ready to do what is good. They must not slander anyone and must avoid quarreling. Instead, they should be gentle and show true humility to everyone.

TITUS 3:1-2, NLT

Get rid of all evil behavior. Be done with all deceit, hypocrisy, jealousy, and all unkind speech.

I PETER 2:1, NLT

When you believe you are a soldier in a culture war, fighting on the side of righteousness, it's easy to rationalize and justify "trench talk." I felt it was my evangelical obligation, if not my right, to "call it like I see it." Cultural warfare and campaign strategies became a constant concern, and my ear was more and more drawn to the emerging media form of conservative talk radio, where apocalyptic scenarios were discussed ad nauseam—especially when it came to the possibility of Democratic political control in Washington, DC. It failed to occur to me that Jesus concerned himself very little with political issues in the way that much of the evangelical community does today. He didn't bring a moral crusade to the hallways of government. He spoke to the hearts behind the system. He worked to change hearts and minds rather than policies and politicians.

Don't think for a moment that the climate in Israel during the time of Jesus was any less politically charged than ours is today. It would not be an overstatement to say it was even more volatile. The tyranny of the Romans was legendary.

They taxed and subjugated the Jewish people, constantly threatened their religious culture, and flaunted their own immoral ways as they expanded their empire. It was an oppressive and ungodly climate, which the Jews detested. They longed to see the Roman government overthrown.

What was Jesus' demeanor in that atmosphere? When we read the Gospels, we get the sense that he sort of shrugged his shoulders as he considered the ruling governments. He certainly wasn't ignoring them, but he knew something they didn't know. Jesus was attuned to and responding from a superior Kingdom.

His lack of aggression toward the Romans drove the zealous Jewish religious folk nuts. But Jesus had a plan. His agenda was not to overthrow the government from the top, but to subvert it from underneath with what he called the Kingdom of Heaven. It would be like yeast worked into dough, or a tiny mustard seed planted in the corner of the garden, that would grow to an enormous size . . . working from the inside out.

The Seduction of Nationalism and Patriotism

Have you ever noticed that people are always talking about changing the world? And just about every generation, at least those that have emerged in the past 150 years, believes it *can* change the world. But rarely does a single movement or event actually have that effect.

Yet it happened in our lifetime.

In the aftermath of 9/11, countless politicians and media

personalities declared that the world would be forever changed by the events of that day. It turns out they were right.

Do you remember the days—and not that long ago—when you could meet friends and family members directly at the airport gate as they exited the plane? How about when you could carry a cooler or large bag into an amusement park, concert, or sporting event without having it searched? And when have we ever been so justifiably concerned about the government snooping into our private affairs?

Terrorists. Roadside bombs. Homeland security. Threats. Drones. TSA. Border patrol. Gun control. These words and phrases have become commonplace in our daily conversations and lives. Freedom in the Land of the Free is not the freedom it used to be. Public life is not the same. Fear encroaches at the edges of our culture.

Have you noticed something else? Military personnel in full fatigues and armament have become commonplace at airports and major public events. Honoring military members at sporting events and concerts, with discounts at restaurants and movie theaters, or giving them privileges such as first to board on commercial airplanes have also become customary.

"Yeah, so what's the problem? Where's your patriotism?"

I realize that touching on this subject is tantamount to poking a sleeping bear. Americans have always been very patriotic. I'm an American—and a Texan. I get that. My father served in the Air Force, and I have uncles and great-uncles who fought in the two World Wars. I am deeply grateful for their bravery and sacrifice. I am thankful for the United States of America and am glad to be a citizen of our great nation. I love our ideals of freedom and equality. I love it that our first instinct as a nation is to rush to the aid of countries that have experienced natural disasters and the like.

But what concerns me about America is how often we violate our own principles in the interest of pragmatism. This happens when we support brutal regimes because "it's in our national interest." It happens when we torture "enemy combatants." It happens when we gloss over our own history and the barbaric ways and means by which our nation's forefathers—whom we label as *godly*—inflicted pain on at least two races of our fellow humans, with little or no brokenness for the treachery involved in those actions.

Patriotism is one thing. Nationalism is a different animal. It is idolatrous. Nationalism places its own interests above the interests of others, often justifying the actions and policies of one nation over another, no matter the cost to the other country and its people.

I'm not shocked when our government engages in such acts because I know that human governments act from human strength. The appalling thing—the heartbreaking thing—is when Bible-toting, Scripture-quoting, listen-only-to-Christian-radio evangelicals applaud and defend such policies and wage heated arguments in defense of them.

My concern is that something subtle, yet very tangible, has taken shape in the hearts and minds of a large number of evangelicals. An American mind-set has largely trumped a Jesusian mind-set—that is, we view life more through the lens of our culture than through the lens of our Creator. To a significant degree, patriotism, party affiliation, and national interests have shaped evangelical Christian thinking to such a degree that it undermines our identity as agents and citizens of a holy nation, the Kingdom of Heaven. This shows itself in a fearful, on-edge population of self-avowed Christ followers who, in the name of security and safety, are just as willing and ready to kill or say "amen" to violence as their neighbors who make no claim whatsoever to being followers of the Prince of Peace.

A close friend of mine once shared with me his firsthand account of a well-known megachurch pastor who gave him a tour of the *bunker* he had built at his home. It was stocked with food, water, guns, and ammunition, in case of an economic apocalypse. When my friend asked what the massive stockpile of ammunition was for, the pastor said it was to fend off people who would try to take his family's food and water. My buddy was stunned. Why would the pastor—the Christ follower and leader of others—not be inclined to leave his life in the hands of the Lord and share his food and water? Whatever happened to the mind-set expressed by the apostle Paul in ACTS 20:24?

> I do not account my life of any value nor as precious to myself, if only I may finish my course and the ministry that I received from the Lord Jesus, to testify to the gospel of the grace of God.

The pastor's attitude is just one example of how "American individualism" has infected the church and become a common evangelical obsession with personal rights to the exclusion of the gospel of Jesus. Not everyone has the disease, mind you, but it is certainly widespread.

History is full of stories of Christ followers running *toward*, not away from, human suffering and tragedy—such as persecutions, plagues, and wars—to the neglect of their own safety and with very real danger to their own lives. But something has changed in the evangelical mind. It's as if we have spiritual amnesia. We've forgotten who we are, where we've come from, and where we're going.

In Galatians 3, the apostle Paul opens with some tough language: "Foolish Galatians! Who has bewitched you?" I can easily imagine a similar approach if Paul were to address the church in the United States today: "Foolish Americans! Who has bewitched you?" Many of our positions on issues such as immigration, the poor, and justifications for war have been formed more from a desire for economic stability, self-preservation, and national interest than from the perspective and edicts of God's Kingdom and the teaching of Jesus. Often, it seems, our arguments are drawn from professing-Christian politicians with questionable theology or media personalities who sprinkle Bible verses on whatever point they're making at the time.

The king of conservative talk radio, Rush Limbaugh, went so far as to accuse Pope Francis of teaching Marxism because of the pope's critique of unfettered capitalism in his paper titled "Evangelii Gaudium" (Joy of the Gospel).[4] And none other than former vice presidential hopeful Sarah Palin declared, "[Pope Francis] had some statements that to me sounded kind of liberal."[5]

Over the past decade or so, a growing number of evangelicals have turned almost devotionally to the daily commentary, advice, and opinions of radio and television personalities. One thing these voices have in common, I've noticed, is the widespread degree to which they are rooted in fear. Constant warnings about "threats to your rights and your future" pepper almost every broadcast. For Christians, this "spirit of fear" should be a red flag that these voices do not represent the wisdom of God (see 2 Timothy 1:7).

Contrary to such dreadful posturing, the phrase "fear not" echoes over and over across the panorama of Scripture. The Lord never leads on the basis of fearfulness, and he certainly doesn't grease the gospel of the Kingdom with fear. Much of what comes from the conservative media pushes evangelicals toward a mind-set of self-preservation to a degree that blinds our minds and closes our hearts to the message and agenda of Jesus. Rather than encouraging us to think in terms of engaging with our culture and reaching the lost, the emphasis is on ways to bunker away from the world and save our own skins. In effect, the evangelical heart has been hijacked.

When evangelicals allow their politics and policies to be shaped by talking heads and talk show hosts, the gospel train runs off the rails. As Yale theology professor Ronald Sider writes, "The absence of any widely accepted, systematic evangelical reflection on politics leads to contradiction, confusion, ineffectiveness, even biblical unfaithfulness in our political work."[6]

In C. S. Lewis's *The Screwtape Letters,* readers eavesdrop on the mentorship of a junior demon as Screwtape trains Wormwood on how to gain the Christian heart:

> Let him begin by treating the Patriotism . . . as a part
> of his religion. Then let him, under the influence
> of partisan spirit, come to regard it as the most
> important part. Then quietly and gradually nurse
> him on to the stage at which the religion becomes
> merely part of the "cause," in which Christianity is
> valued chiefly because of the excellent arguments it
> can produce. . . . Once you have made the World
> an end, and faith a means, you have almost won
> your man, and it makes very little difference what
> kind of worldly end he is pursuing. Provided that
> meetings, pamphlets, policies, movements, causes,
> and crusades, matter more to him than prayers and
> sacraments and charity, he is ours—and the more
> "religious" (on those terms) the more securely ours.[7]

Excessive patriotism effectively shuts down our love and concern for others. When this happens on a wide scale among Christians, the *Good News* in the *Good News people* goes undelivered, and the way of salvation becomes obscured. When we place labels on people, calling them deadbeats, worthless, scum, cowards, traitors, etc., we disqualify *ourselves* as vessels or conduits of God's love, compassion, and grace to the world. We dam up the river of life in our own hearts, leaving us little to offer a parched world other than a stagnant pool of condemnation.

In an article titled "Where Is the Love?" *New York Times* writer Nicholas Kristof reported on a Princeton University research project that found "when research subjects hooked up to neuroimaging machines look at photos of the poor and homeless, their brains often react as if they are seeing *things*, not people. Her analysis suggests that Americans sometimes react to poverty not with sympathy but with revulsion."[8]

I know for a fact—through discussions and reading web postings—that a multitude of evangelicals, who staunchly declare their allegiance to Jesus, have outright hatred in their hearts for the "enemies of America." How contrary is that to the "perfect love" that "*casts out* fear"? (1 John 4:18, emphasis added). This is this same *perfect love* that drove Jesus to give his life for us; the same *perfect love* that should be in our hearts, compelling us to love others . . . including *enemy* others.

If we want America to be a Christian nation, why wouldn't we want to act Christianly toward our enemies?

Apart from mottos on our coins and currency and patriotic songs invoking the blessing of God, when it comes to actually acting on faith in Jesus and his ways, the idea of any nation being *Christian* is deeply flawed. So many evangelical Christians who insist we have always been a Christian nation unconscionably dismiss the teachings of Christ when it comes to inconvenient decisions or issues that confront our nation. Were we a Christian nation when our forefathers prospered from the blood, sweat, and tears of African slaves? Were we a Christian nation when we stole land, pillaged, and broke treaty after treaty with the Native American tribes? We need to ask ourselves what it even means to declare a nation as *Christian*.

I find no evidence there has ever been a legitimately *Christian* nation, and I find it hard to imagine that God ever expected there to be one. We live in a fallen world, and governments formed within this broken system will operate as best they know how—and that includes using force at times to maintain order. Though Jesus rebuked Peter for using a sword to defend him in the garden of Gethsemane, we find that God sanctions the use of the sword in the hands of governments to preserve law and order (see Romans 13:1-7). This is why I agree with Greg Boyd, who wrote *The Myth of a Christian Religion*:

> The fact is that no government or nation in history has ever looked remotely like Jesus. None has ever made it a policy *not* to forcefully resist criminals or enemies. None has ever committed itself to blessing criminals, serving enemies, and refusing to retaliate when people or nations do it wrong. Nor has any political regime ever established laws to return evil with good, turn the other cheek, or lend to their enemies without expecting anything in return. Yet these are what Jesus and his Kingdom are all about.[9]

The fruit of the Kingdom of God bears the likeness of Jesus. "It always looks like Jesus—loving, serving, and sacrificing himself for all people, including his enemies."[10] When our attitudes and actions depart from the character of Christ, it's a good bet we've walked out of the sphere of the Kingdom of Heaven. I often think of this whenever I see comments of lament from evangelicals about stories of American soldiers who have lost their lives in battle. It is good, right, and in accord with the words of Jesus that we mourn with those who mourn. But rarely do I find similar comments of sadness over the lost lives of non-Americans on the same battlefields. The distinctions we draw on the relative value of human lives reflects the nationalism in our hearts.

Do we actually believe that an American life is worth more than an Afghan life? Do we believe God weeps with us over the deaths of a dozen American soldiers, while simultaneously thinking, *That's the way it goes*, about the deaths of several dozen Iraqi civilians or "enemy" soldiers? Although Jesus told us to "seek first the kingdom of God and his righteousness,"[11] too many evangelicals, it seems, have become American Christians rather than Christian Americans.

I recall the time I visited Mount Rushmore, in the Black Hills of South Dakota. On the drive there, I asked my local host about the current status of the Lakota Indians, who still live on reservations there. He told me they are a people who, to this day, are psychologically and financially decimated as a result of the American conquering doctrine of Manifest Destiny.

The Lakota consider the Black Hills sacred, and they were once protected as part of a treaty with the American government—that is, until trespassing prospectors found gold there. Retaliation by the Lakota against these incursions marked the beginning of the end for the tribe's independence. After their ultimate defeat by American troops, after a running series of battles, including the Battle of the Little Bighorn, the Lakota were confined to reservations, prevented from hunting buffalo (which were hunted and slaughtered nearly to extinction to eradicate the Lakota's primary food source), and left with little choice but to accept the government's food distribution. For well over one hundred years, these once proud and self-sufficient people have been a broken society

For me, the grandeur of Mount Rushmore was lost. I couldn't get past the heartbreaking thought of how the Lakota people must feel seeing the faces of white American heroes literally carved into their sacred hills, perpetually looking down on them. Less than five minutes after arriving, I told my host I was ready to leave.

When *Rights* Go Wrong

Knowing that I'm a card-carrying Texan, it may not surprise you to learn that I'm also a gun-owning Texan. I still have the little 410 shotgun my dad gave me for Christmas when I was twelve years old, along with his 12-gauge shotgun, a .22 pistol, and a couple of other pistols. Back in my high school days, my buddies and I parked our trucks in the school parking lot with shotguns and rifles in plain sight, hanging on gun racks in the back window. Of course, that was ages ago. It seems almost mythical now.

The constitutional right to keep and bear arms is something I appreciate and exercise. I don't believe this right is wrong, but I certainly believe we can hold it with the wrong attitude. And many people do. The right to own a firearm is not something to flaunt, or that a Christ follower should passionately defend as if it were a *biblical mandate*. If US law happens to change in my lifetime and I'm required to turn in my guns, I will regretfully do so. I will not bunker inside my house and scream about my "God-given right to bear arms." But from what I've heard from many devoted American Christians, they would not let go quite so easily.

You often hear the mantra "when they pry it from my cold, dead fingers" uttered by evangelicals when the subject of gun control comes up. My heart sank recently when one of my friends (whom in many ways I consider a far better example of a Jesus person than I am) told me he would fill any policeman or government official full of bullet holes if they tried to enter his home to confiscate his guns. "Without an ounce of guilt," he added.

My belief in this particular friend makes it hard for me to think he could actually follow through on such a threat. But the passion in his voice and the set in his jaw when he said it was nonetheless unfathomable, coming from such a devout Christian. Somehow, it's hard to imagine those same words coming from the lips of Jesus.

My intention here is not to take a stand on a particular

set of issues. My burden is to see the hearts of evangelical Christians square with the heart of Jesus. The big question for everyone who claims the name of Jesus is this: *Is my heart right?* Is my allegiance to an earthly empire (such as the US of A) or to the Kingdom of God?

Our identity as Americans must bow to our identity as citizens of a higher realm. When someone who professes faith in Jesus is as callous or bloodthirsty in the name of "rights" as his nonbelieving neighbor, something is dreadfully amiss— the heart of Jesus and the message of the gospel have yet to convert that person. The apostle Paul instructs us to think and live differently:

> If then you have been raised with Christ, seek the
> things that are above, where Christ is, seated at
> the right hand of God. Set your minds on things
> that are above, not on things that are on earth. . . .
> Here there is not Greek and Jew, circumcised and
> uncircumcised, barbarian, Scythian, slave, free; but
> Christ is all, and in all.
>
> COLOSSIANS 3:1-2, 11

Paul is telling us to fix our minds on the Kingdom of Heaven and to stop categorizing people according to nationality, religious affiliation, or social class. In the Kingdom of Heaven, there is neither Greek, nor Jew, nor Afghan, nor Iranian, nor American. To think anything less is earthly mindedness.

When we enter the Kingdom of God, our old identity is

changed. Part and parcel with this change is a reordering of our allegiances. In our evangelical churches, we have forgotten—or most likely were never taught—the weightiness of how the Kingdom of Heaven is to change our worldview and how we live our lives here and now. We sing the songs declaring that we have tossed away our own crowns, but have we really?

Who Are You?

The word *kingdom* is a conjunction of two words: *king* and *domain*. It refers to the realm of a king's dominion, including his edicts, ethics, commands, and pursuits. Citizens in a kingdom must abide by the decrees of their king and give him their allegiance. And they are not to follow or obey any rival monarch who would seek to usurp the authority and decrees of the reigning king. To do so would be treason. A kingdom refers to the realm in which what the king wants done gets done. It is the jurisdiction of his effective will.

During the early years of the Christian church, the Roman Empire was the reigning earthly kingdom. Caesar's decrees were the first and final word. As the empire expanded, it established colonies in territories beyond Rome. Though many of these outposts were hundreds of miles from the capital in Rome, they were nonetheless Roman territory and represented Roman rule and lifestyle. And even the most far-flung citizens of Rome were expected to conform to Roman standards.

The United States of America, of course, grew out of what were largely British colonies. The colonists had their ancestral roots in Great Britain and considered themselves citizens and subjects of King George III. Their ultimate breakaway from the lordship of the king of England ignited the struggle for American independence.

To be a disciple of Jesus and a believer in the gospel of the Kingdom of God means we have become citizens and colonists of heaven. As colonists, we must adapt ourselves to the circumstances of our adopted home while establishing a new society, an extension and reflection of our true homeland. This means our primary allegiance must be to the Kingdom of Heaven.

> You are a chosen race, a royal priesthood, a *holy*
> *nation*, a people for his own possession.
> 1 PETER 2:9 (italics added)

> *Our citizenship is in heaven*, and from it we await
> a Savior, the Lord Jesus Christ.
> PHILIPPIANS 3:20 (italics added)

Close to a century ago, Methodist theologian E. Stanley Jones wrote:

> If we could get men to respond to the emotion of
> the ideal of the Kingdom of God as we can get them
> to respond to the emotion of the national ideal;
> if we could get men to have a patriotism to the
> Kingdom comparable to what they give to a national

patriotism, then a new social heredity would be
brought to bear upon the world and the world could
be changed in an incredibly short time.[12]

In the context of the Roman Empire, the most appalling
statement the early Christians could have made was, "Jesus
is Lord." Those three words were downright scandalous
and carried enormous implications. We've lost the outrage
of those words. By asserting Jesus as their Lord, the first
Christians declared that Caesar was *not* their lord and ruler.
They would pay their taxes and abstain from corrupt speech
against the emperor, but any demands he placed on them
that contradicted the commands of Jesus would be shunned.
The Kingdom of Heaven trumped the Roman Empire. The
Christians identified themselves as citizens *in* Rome, but not
of Rome. They were citizens of heaven stationed in Rome.

By announcing that the Kingdom of Heaven was within
reach, Jesus declared open access to all that heaven had to
offer. He pointed his followers to a *higher* way of living and
thinking. This may be why we traditionally think of heaven
as "up there." The biblical notion of heaven is that it is a
higher *realm*, a superior dimension. It is "up" in the sense
that it is above all others.

Jesus did not say that the Kingdom of Heaven was just
then coming into existence. This is why it is erroneous to
say that we *build* the Kingdom or *expand* the Kingdom.
Jesus never uses such language. He speaks of *receiving* or

entering into the Kingdom of Heaven. His message is that the Kingdom is now *accessible*. Dallas Willard writes:

> When he announced that the "governance" or rule of God had become available to human beings, he was primarily referring to what *he* could do for people, God acting with him. But he was also offering to communicate this same "rule of God" to others who would receive and learn it from him. He was himself the evidence for the truth of his announcement about the availability of God's kingdom, or governance, to ordinary human existence.[13]

In directing us to pray, "Thy kingdom come," Jesus wasn't telling us we needed to pray for the Kingdom to come into existence. He wanted us to pray for it to *overtake* all earthly domains—every personal, social, and political arena. Other kingdoms still exist—earthly kingdoms, the kingdom of darkness, and our own personal fiefdoms—and the tension between all of these is what scholars refer to as the "already and not yet" of the Kingdom of Heaven. It means that God's reign is *already* breaking in (now) and will one day completely sweep over every earthly kingdom, but it has *not yet* been fully realized.

Likewise for us as Christians, there are some areas of our lives in which we have "entered into" the Kingdom of Heaven and submitted to the reign of God, and other areas in which we continue to maintain our own rule.

Too often, the ethics of Jesus have been looked at as impractical for the *real* world. Consequently, much of what Jesus plainly taught us has effectively been tossed aside. It's as if we believe we are smarter than Jesus about the practicalities of life in the twenty-first century. Author Tom Krattenmaker, who is also the religion columnist for *USA Today*, draws upon this thought when he asks:

> Could it be that on certain key issues, Jesus' most vocal representatives—people who will tell you that faith guides every aspect of their lives—have been basing their politics not on the Bible but on something else? . . . In 2008, when "enhanced interrogation" stood center stage in the headlines and political arguments, Jones's polling found that 57 percent of white evangelicals in the South believed torture could be justified, in contrast with the 48 percent of the general public found to support torture in an earlier poll by the Pew Research Center. But the real lesson lay in this data point: the evangelicals surveyed . . . were far more likely to be basing their pro-torture stance on life experience and common sense (44 percent) than Christian teaching (28 percent). In other words . . . the segment of the population presumably the most serious about living the Christian life is disinclined to be guided by the Bible on one of the central moral questions of the day. . . . [A] slightly different

result . . . emerged when the pollsters tweaked
the question and challenged the survey takers
to reapproach the issue with the Bible in mind,
particularly its "do unto others as you would have
them do unto you" precept. A slight majority then
agreed that torture should never be used.[14]

We see the same pattern in other current topics of debate:

A 2010 poll . . . found just 12 percent of white
evangelicals indicated that their religious beliefs had
a major influence on their views about immigration
policy. Similarly, just 13 percent said their faith
was the biggest influence on their views about
government aid to the poor.[15]

Let that sink in. Most Christians have little understanding
of what Scripture says about immigrants—those whom the
Bible calls *strangers* and *aliens*. But the Bible has a lot to
say on the matter. Many evangelicals can instantly parrot
viewpoints and arguments from Hannity, Beck, O'Reilly,
Stewart, Matthews, or Maddow, but they have few or no
talking points from Isaiah, Ezekiel, Jeremiah, or James.

How can evangelicals be so vocal, energized, and stirred
up about issues and yet take positions so feebly informed
by the gospel of Jesus? How can we allow our attitudes and
perspectives to be shaped by national and cultural interests
rather than by biblical and eternal concerns? This is why we

need to be *re-evangelized*. We need to repledge our allegiance to the Kingdom of Heaven.

Any gospel that says it's about going to heaven falls far short of the "on earth as it is in heaven" gospel that Jesus taught—the gospel of the in-breaking Kingdom of God at hand. Front-page headline issues such as dealing with our enemies, immigrants, and the poor are tangible and concrete invitations for followers of Jesus to either *enter into* the Kingdom of Heaven or *remain on the outskirts*.

When there is inconsistency or incongruity between our professed beliefs and our attitudes and actions, it creates cognitive dissonance—not only for us, but also for the watching world, which is left unchanged and unchallenged by the ways and means of Jesus. Many non-Christians are left scratching their heads at evangelicals whose ideologies deny the very Jesus they claim to follow. And this inconsistency can be found across the political spectrum, as author Jonathan Merritt observes:

> Those on the right don't seem to wrestle with whether the Prince of Peace would unflinchingly support war or how following a God who cares about the poor would produce disciples who seem to blame the poor for their many woes (and ours). Those on the left are correct to highlight care for "the least of these" but often brush over the millions of aborted children who undoubtedly fall under that label.[16]

Where to Stand

The wisdom of the world is by its very nature antithetical to the wisdom of Jesus. The world tells us to call "shotgun" and grab the front seat. Jesus tells us to choose to sit in the back. The world tells us that the smartest and strongest among us are the greatest. Jesus tells us the greatest are the most humble servants in our midst. The world tells us to rule with power. Jesus tells us to rule with humility—which is true power exercised under control. These are examples of what makes the Kingdom of Jesus "not of this world" (John 18:36).

When we distance our minds and hearts from a thoroughly biblical understanding of God's ways—which in turn shapes our worldview about current events, societal struggles, and political positions—we undermine our ability to gain a Kingdom-of-Heaven perspective on these issues, and this holds others back as well.

When our go-to sources of "wisdom" on current events are politicians, news anchors, and celebrity pundits, we prove by our actions that we really don't believe in a biblical standard that touches our day-to-day lives in the "real world," and we relegate Jesus to the role of wise (but essentially irrelevant) teacher. To put it another way, when our gospel is all about salvation and getting to heaven, we tend to overlook what Jesus says about living our lives by Kingdom principles in the here and now.

Before the Good News of the in-breaking Kingdom of Heaven can have its transformative effect on our broader culture, it must first arrest the hearts and minds of those who profess to follow Jesus. "But this cannot come about," writes Dallas Willard, "unless what Jesus himself believed, practiced, and taught *makes sense* to us. And his message must come to us free of the deadening legalisms, political slogan-eering, and dogmatic traditionalisms long proven by history to be soul-crushing dead ends."[17]

For starters, we must understand that the in-breaking Kingdom of Heaven is a *movement of the Holy Spirit in the world*, not a top-down, rule-making monarchy. As professor of Christian ethics Glen Stassen explains it:

> Scholars agree that the kingdom of God in Jesus' teaching is not a place, like the Kingdom of Monaco, but a happening. It means God's reign, God's presence, God's coming to deliver us and reign over us. In our present-day language, it is probably clearer to speak of "the reign of God."
>
> Jesus' language about reigning did not mean that Israel would rule over other nations, or that any human empire with a king would be established over other nations. He meant that God was coming to redeem or deliver us from our present mess and would reign instead.[18]

How does God intend to reign? What is the *ethos* or *nature* of his Kingdom? Jesus said it would not be through human power and domination, but by his disciples taking on the mantle of *sacrificial servanthood*. His plan was to make disci-ple-making disciples, who would train up succeeding genera-tions of disciples in every people group in the world. But in our day, this plan, commonly called the Great Commission (Matthew 28:19-20), has effectively been reduced to a plan of *conversion* (i.e., how to get to heaven) rather than a plan to *make disciples* who will join with the mission of God's in-breaking Kingdom on earth.

Think about how Jesus interacted with his original disci-ples—not only with the twelve, or even just the seventy-two, but with everyone who followed him during his time on earth. His teaching wasn't focused on how to get to heaven, but on how to live *heavenly*. Jesus taught them how to *live their lives*—in the midst of Roman-dominated Palestine—according to the principles and practices of the Kingdom of Heaven, which affect *every aspect* of life.

In his book *Living the Sermon on the Mount*, Glen Stassen addresses our tendency to compartmentalize our lives:

> Some people make the mistake of splitting life into two realms: the temporal and political on the one hand, which supposedly do not concern Jesus, and the world of "religious" things on the other, which do matter to Jesus. But this makes Jesus' teaching mostly irrelevant for much of life. Jesus did not split life in that way. . . . He affirmed that God is Lord over *all* of life, not just religious or inner or individual or spiritual life.[19]

The revolution Jesus ushered in was neither political nor nationalistic. He demonstrated no allegiance to or preference for any particular nation's agenda—including the nation of Israel. In every instance in history in which people have attempted to impose their own ideas of what God is for or against by the use of might and power, they have both "trivialized the Kingdom and denied its essential character."[20]

Not Like You Think

We evangelicals often laugh at the disciples' blunders, but we have a propensity for thinking the same way they did during their apprenticeship with Jesus. They were always asking when the Kingdom was going to come and what their status or position would be in it. Jesus repeatedly emphasized that his Kingdom was not going to look like any kingdom they had seen, or like any kingdom they longed to see established in his name. The disciples were certain that Jesus would overthrow the Roman government and impose his own rule of law, sitting on a throne in Jerusalem with the disciples as his cabinet. Too often we are fixated on the wrong questions. Renowned scholar N. T. Wright says,

> The New Testament, true to its Old Testament roots,
> regularly insists that the major, central, framing
> question is that of God's purpose of rescue and
> re-creation for the whole world, the entire cosmos.
> . . . The question ought to be, *How will God's
> new creation come?* and then, *How will we humans*

*contribute to that renewal of creation and to the fresh
projects that the creator God will launch in his new
world?* The choice before humans would then be
framed differently: Are you going to worship the
creator God and discover thereby what it means
to become fully and gloriously human, reflecting
his powerful, healing, transformative love into
the world? Or are you going to worship the world
as it is, boosting your corruptible humanness by
gaining power or pleasure from forces within the
world but merely contributing thereby to your own
dehumanization and the further corruption of the
world itself?[21]

To shine as good news people, Christians must abandon the
"righteous meanness" for which we've gained a reputation.
Let us recover *grace* and *truth* and *love* and be servers of kind
words and actions. Nothing less than the perfect love of Jesus
will cast out the fear stirred up by pundits and politicians in
our society. By pledging our allegiance to the Kingdom of
God, we interrupt and circumvent the common ways of our
culture. In effect, we rewire the circuit boards in our hearts
and tune ourselves to a new frequency. Reframing our identity
as citizens of heaven is hard work. And it is *heart* work. The
ways of Jesus are both *impractical* and *inconvenient*. Along
with his promise of eternal life, his nonsensical ideas about
life here and right now convey the beauty of the Kingdom of
Heaven and are what make the gospel good news.

QUESTIONS FOR REFLECTION

1. In what ways has your citizenship of your earthly homeland co-opted your status as a citizen of heaven?

2. Have you allowed fear-driven news to overshadow and shape the good news of the Kingdom of Heaven in your mind and heart? If so, how?

3. Who are your "enemies" right now, and what would you like to see happen to them?

4. Drawing from the teachings of Jesus in the Gospels, if he were an American citizen today, what would be his stance and voice on the political issues in the news?

5. In what ways has this chapter challenged your identity as an evangelical Christian?

4
RECONCILE

The Pharisee stood by himself and prayed this prayer:
"I thank you, God, that I am not a sinner like everyone else."

LUKE 18:11, NLT

But when the teachers of religious law who were Pharisees
saw him eating with tax collectors and other sinners, they
asked his disciples, "Why does he eat with such scum?"

MARK 2:16, NLT

God loves us as we are, and not as we should be.
Because none of us are as we should be.

BRENNAN MANNING

OUR FAMILY used to have a small hobby farm with a few horses. I bought alfalfa hay for them from a local rancher named Don, who was a prototypical good ol' boy Baptist deacon. He loved to recite the mantra, "I don't drink, and I don't chew, and I don't run with girls that do." On the dashboard of his pickup truck, right next to a pair of greasy work gloves, a ball-peen hammer, and various leftover fast-food wrappers, a three-inch-thick Bible was a permanent fixture.

Late one summer afternoon, after unloading a delivery of hay, as Don and I sat on the tailgate of his truck drinking iced tea, he smugly grinned and told me he had received an invitation from a local contractor to an annual end-of-summer picnic.

Don shook his head and said, "Jimmy sends me one of those invitations every single year. And just like always, I won't be going."

When he mentioned that most all of the local neighbors, farmers, and contractors would be there, I asked why he never went.

"Because they'll have beer there, and he knows where I stand on drinkin'. It would hurt my *witness*. I'm a Christian," he said matter-of-factly, "and if Jesus wouldn't be there, I won't be either."

I picked up a stalk of straw from the truck bed and pointed to the cab. "Well, Don, you might want to take another look at that Bible of yours on the dashboard. I think you'll find that Jesus would possibly be the first one to show up at Jimmy's picnic. In fact, if the keg ran dry, he would probably make sure it was refilled with the best beer in St. Louis."

Don's mouth dropped to his belt. "Well, that's just crazy," he said, "I've never read anything like that in the Bible."

Once our ideas of "living the Christian life" have become pickled in the juices of our own moralizing, it's easy to overlook what Scripture actually says about how Jesus interacted with people. Here's just one example from the Gospels:

As Jesus reclined at table in the house, behold, many tax collectors and sinners came and were reclining

with Jesus and his disciples. And when the Pharisees
saw this, they said to his disciples, "Why does your
teacher eat with tax collectors and sinners?"

MATTHEW 9:10-11

And here's how it affected his "witness":

The Son of Man came eating and drinking, and
they say, "Look at him! A glutton and a drunkard,
a friend of tax collectors and sinners!"

MATTHEW 11:19

But here's the final word, from Jesus' perspective: "Wisdom
is justified by her deeds."[1]

With all Don's concern about his "witness for Christ," it
seemed the only thing he accomplished was to send a message to others that he thought he was too good for them.

Compare Don's approach with that of my buddy Hugh
Halter, who planted a church in Denver about seven or eight
years ago. Within the first year, Hugh's next-door neighbor
became quite involved in the church and was clearly on a
journey toward believing. That didn't sit well with the neighbor's husband, however, and he seized upon the opportunity
to send a message to the interloping pastor.

One day while Hugh was mowing his grass, he looked
up to see his burly neighbor standing on his deck next door
with a beer in one hand and the other hand flipping Hugh
the bird—yes, the nasty finger.

As you might appreciate, Hugh was dumbfounded. What are you supposed to do with that? Understand, Hugh is not your ordinary, run-of-the-mill pastor type. He's far from spit-and-polished and makes no effort to uphold the stereotypical image of a pastor.

After taking a couple more passes with the mower across his lawn while mulling over the proper response—with his neighbor holding a steady, one-finger salute all the while—Hugh took action. He stopped, released the mower handle, and held up not one, but both middle fingers. Hugh saw his neighbor's bird and raised him one.

Clearly this was not the response the man expected from his neighbor the pastor. It was a standoff. With three middle fingers hovering in the air, not a word was spoken for several seconds. Then the neighbor slowly cracked a smile and started to laugh. "Dude, you wanna drink?" he asked. This was the beginning of what has become a wonderful friendship with a guy who is now a member of Hugh's faith community.

Hear me: I am *not* advocating or promoting "flip off your neighbor" evangelism. Still, Hugh used a whimsical response to reach this guy where he lived. He didn't *stoop* to his level. He simply *met* him on his level.

Friendship with the World

In the eyes of the religious establishment of his day, Jesus said and did some pretty outrageous things. He *still* does. Just read the Beatitudes (Matthew 5:3-12) and see if he doesn't offend your twenty-first-century sensibilities on numerous fronts when you try to *apply* what he commands. Jesus is just too impractical for the "real world." He was certainly beyond reason for the religious leaders of his day.

In all of history, there have been no more astute adherents of the Scriptures than the Pharisees. For Jesus, though, just *knowing* the Bible was never enough. He wanted people to understand the *heart* and *intent* behind the Scriptures. He constantly rebuked the scholars of his day for obsessing over the letter of the law, including punctuation and syntax, while missing the overall *purpose* the Holy Spirit had in mind from the outset.

> What sorrow awaits you Pharisees! For you are
> careful to tithe even the tiniest income from your
> herb gardens, but you ignore justice and the love of
> God. You should tithe, yes, but do not neglect the
> more important things.
>
> LUKE 11:42, NLT

The King James Version of this passage says, "Ye . . . pass over judgment and the love of God." It wasn't that these religious devotees disagreed with or rejected justice and the love of God; they simply *passed them over* and moved on to matters they considered more significant. But Jesus said the things they passed over were "the more important things." Like so many religious people today, the Pharisees were more passionate about judging others than seeking justice for others.

Previously, we looked at the story of the Good Samaritan. We would do well to take a second look, this time focusing on another key point Jesus wants us to see:

A man was going down from Jerusalem to Jericho, and he fell among robbers, who stripped him and beat him and departed, leaving him half dead. Now by chance a priest was going down that road, and when he saw him he passed by on the other side. So likewise a Levite, when he came to the place and saw him, passed by on the other side.[2]

Similar to "passing over" or neglecting the more important things, we see another type of *passing over* here. This is the sin of holding ourselves back from others by "passing over to the other side" in their hour of need. John Wesley, the famed Methodist preacher, said:

One great reason why the rich in general have so little sympathy for the poor, is, because they so seldom visit them. Hence it is, that, according to the common observation, one part of the world does not know what the other suffers. Many of them do not know, because they do not care to know: they keep out of the way of knowing it; and then plead their voluntary ignorance, as an excuse for their hardness of heart. "Indeed, sir," (said a person of large substance,) "I am a very

compassionate man. But to tell you the truth, I
do not know anybody in the world that is in want."
How did this come to pass? Why, he took good
care to keep out of their way. And if he fell upon
any of them unawares, "he passed over on the
other side."[3]

Relationally, I spent the first couple decades of my life as
a Christ follower in a Christian bubble. During my younger years as a believer, I heard certain verses quoted as proof
texts to enforce the idea of not having relationships with
non-Christians. If they showed up at church, that was fine,
but to join a bowling league, play on a softball team, or play
cards with a bunch of unsaved dudes? No way. That would
be compromise.

I read Scriptures such as these and took them to mean I
should not have "worldly" friendships:

You adulterers! Don't you realize that friendship
with the world makes you an enemy of God? I say
it again: If you want to be a friend of the world, you
make yourself an enemy of God.

JAMES 4:4, NLT

Do not love the world or the things in the world. If
anyone loves the world, the love of the Father is not
in him.

I JOHN 2:15

But I failed to read these verses *in context*. Reading the text before and after these verses makes it abundantly clear that the "world" spoken of is not the *people* of the world, but the *system* of the world. The apostles are not instructing readers to abandon their friends; they are speaking of not loving the greed and selfish ambition that seek to drive us all. It is this *worldly system* we are called out of.

On the other hand, in the following verse, "world" is understood to mean the *people* of the world.

> For God so loved the world, that he gave his only Son, that whoever believes in him should not perish but have eternal life.
>
> JOHN 3:16

In fact, there is quite an unexpected twist to be found in the apostle Paul's first letter to the church in Corinth. He tells the church to disassociate with immoral people. But he is not speaking of immoral non-Christians. Paul makes it clear he is referring to immoral Christians. Read Eugene Peterson's paraphrase of 1 Corinthians 5:9-13:

> I wrote you in my earlier letter that you shouldn't make yourselves at home among the sexually promiscuous. I didn't mean that you should have nothing at all to do with outsiders of that sort. Or with crooks, whether blue- or white-collar. Or with spiritual phonies, for that matter. You'd have to leave

the world entirely to do that! But I *am* saying that you shouldn't act as if everything is just fine when a friend who claims to be a Christian is promiscuous or crooked, is flip with God or rude to friends, gets drunk or becomes greedy and predatory. You can't just go along with this, treating it as acceptable behavior. I'm not responsible for what the *outsiders* do, but don't we have some responsibility for those within our community of believers? God decides on the outsiders, but we need to decide when our brothers and sisters are out of line and, if necessary, clean house.[4]

Getting to Know You

Our family raised chickens for a while, primarily for the eggs. On a couple of occasions, we had to kill a rooster that had become too aggressive. I say "we," but the truth is, my wife did it. I couldn't bring myself to do the deed. I could never butcher our chickens because we had raised them from hatchlings. I saw them every day—feeding, watering, and sheltering them. It may sound silly, but I couldn't bear the thought of killing these animals I had cared for on a daily basis.

You may be wondering if I have a problem eating chicken at a restaurant or purchased from a store. I don't. But something has certainly changed. Almost every time I eat chicken or see my wife preparing it, I think of that animal's life. And when I see stories about the horrendous conditions and treatment of these wonderful creatures at the hands of large farms and producers, my heart aches and my blood boils. The same goes for the meat-producing industry as a whole. Most of us give little or no consideration to the desire to live that every animal has. Before we had our own chickens, I never gave a second thought to the lives of these creatures.

When we keep our distance from a person or a state of affairs, our hearts remain far less open and touched than if we were to move near the situation. Anthropologists call this effect *abstraction*. I'm convinced that many Christians today have hardened hearts and angry words for certain types of people they consider to be on "the other side," the *wrong side*. They don't want to look at the brokenness they happen upon. They choose to avoid it by crossing the street, changing the channel on the TV remote, or diverting their eyes as they pass by. But it's impossible to follow the pattern of the Good Samaritan—or the example of Jesus—if we cross the street to avoid what is in front of us. After all, the Samaritan is the one Jesus said we should imitate.

Martin Luther King Jr. said, "Men often hate each other because they fear each other, and they fear each other because they don't know each other. They don't know each other because they can't communicate with each other, and they can't communicate with each other because they are separated from each other."[5]

When my daughters were teenagers, they both worked at McDonald's. One afternoon, I arrived a few minutes early to pick up Caitlin. As she was finishing her shift, I sat in a booth, surfing the Internet, not far from the cash register where she was stationed.

A middle-aged man walked in and placed an order with Caitlin. When it arrived, he was dissatisfied with something and began to berate her, telling her she was incompetent and that was why she worked at McDonald's. I immediately stood up, and I'm pretty sure it took three or four angels to keep me at my booth and prevent me from making hamburger out of the guy. The store manager was a "customer is always right" policy enforcer, and I didn't want to endanger Caitlin's job by intervening. Remaining silent was one of the hardest things I've ever had to do.

When I dine at any type of restaurant today and the server is a young woman, I can't help but see my daughters in her. I am no longer *abstracted* from these women, even though I don't know them, and it has a huge effect on how I treat them.

One afternoon, I had lunch at a fast-food restaurant with a colleague and a young man we were interviewing for a position in our training program. We were seated in a booth, and I overheard the store manager say to a young employee, "You've been here three weeks; I'm ready to conduct your employee evaluation."

For the past half hour, this young lady had come by our table several times to see if we needed anything. Her demeanor was superb. She made us feel as if we were eating at a nice, full-service restaurant.

When I heard the manager say he was ready to review the

server's performance, my immediate thought was, *I wish he knew how outstanding she is from the perspective of a customer.* But I was stuck on the inside seat in the booth, and we were deep into our interview. It would've been really inconvenient for me to say anything to the manager.

But I couldn't shake it. Every time I glanced over my shoulder toward the teenage server, I saw my daughters. Finally, I couldn't take it anymore. I excused myself from the interview and approached the table where the manager was conducting his employee review.

"Excuse me. Are you the store manager?" I asked.

"Yes, how can I help you?" he replied.

Usually when a customer asks for the manager, it isn't to share something positive. This man's face told me he was bracing for a complaint.

I said, "I couldn't help overhearing your conversation with this young lady, and I wanted you to know that she has treated my friends and me like kings."

As I was talking, the girl smiled from ear to ear, dipping her chin in modesty. The manager immediately broke into a huge smile. I told him that, if she were available, I would hire her away from him in a second. He laughed and said, "Oh, no! She's not available."

Identifying the girl at the restaurant with my own daughters made all the difference. I didn't see her as a nonperson. Her hopes, dreams, struggles, and desires reached my heart simply because I knew someone like her. That's why Jesus said if we are kind or neglectful to "the *least of these*," we have been kind or neglectful to him.[6] He *identified* with people. Likewise, for us, abstractions fade when we identify with the plight of others.

My buddy Brad Brisco and his wife, Mischele, are revangelicals. They have chosen not to cross over into abstraction, choosing instead to identify with those in need. Rather than taking a *fighting* stance as pro-lifers, or joining Christian picketers to shout down abortion doctors and the women who go to them for their services, they chose to get close to a young woman who had a crisis pregnancy. Their youngest son, Caleb, was adopted at birth after they developed a relationship with his teenage mother. Twelve years later, they became a foster family and began taking in other children who needed a safe and loving home.

Their fostering journey began with a question their family consistently asked each other: "In light of the gifts and resources God has given us, how can we touch our neighborhood and the world we are sent into?"

One day it occurred to them that a room in their house they had converted into a home office was almost never used. They decided to switch it back into a bedroom in order to be in a better position to welcome others into their home. This led to their getting involved in "respite care" and "family preservation" services. Both of these programs are about providing *rest* for parents (in most cases, single mothers) and children. The difference between the two is that *respite* involves children who are already in the system (such as when a foster family needs a break), whereas *family preservation* works with families that need assistance to help them stay together so they don't end up in the foster system.

The Briscos also made their home available for "police protective custody," which provides a safe home where children can stay for up to seventy-two hours while the police investigate a potentially dangerous situation at home. In a few instances, the children are eventually returned to their homes; but more often they are moved to a family member's home or are placed in the foster care system until the family can get healthy enough to care for them. Brad told me, "This is short-term, but it provides a wonderful opportunity to show love to children who come from very difficult situations."

The selfish side of respite, he says, is that you can schedule when your family is willing and able to take a child into your home. "It can be a wonderful ministry to single moms who simply need someone to come alongside them, if only for one weekend a month."

After opening their home to more than sixty children over a two-year period, Brad and Mischele adopted the first little girl they had fostered eighteen months earlier, when she was a two-year-old. Chloe had traveled throughout the foster system during that time, before she came back into Brad and Mischele's life. Just shy of her fourth birthday, she officially and forever became a Brisco.

Too many evangelicals verbally condemn their "enemies" or "others" without having even one relationship with an individual from those communities. Woe to anyone who makes condemning comments to Mischele Brisco about women who are considering an abortion or have had one. She'll want to know about that person's relationship with someone facing an abortion decision and how he or she has offered tangible assistance to that woman in crisis. Mischele is not just "pro-life," she is proactive and pro-make-a-life on the issue.

When we make snide and belittling remarks about gays, lesbians, Muslims, immigrants, women who have had an abortion, etc., without having a genuine relationship with real people in those communities or situations, we set ourselves up as self-righteous judges and not the redeemed-by-the-blood-of-Christ Good News people we are meant to be.

Bob Roberts has been a friend and mentor of mine for years. Shortly after American troops invaded Afghanistan, he took me there to scout a village for my church to fund a medical clinic and school. Bob pastors a Texas megachurch but spends much of his time in some of the most hostile environments across the globe. Specifically speaking of the attitude of evangelicals toward Muslims, he writes:

> Our negative feelings are often matched by insensitive actions. . . . Many of us are in the habit of speaking *about* others, rather than *to* them or *with* them. We know how to speak our tribal language, but not how to speak to other tribes. Neither do we realize sometimes how we are coming across. When I visit Christian websites that attempt to evangelize other groups, I try to imagine myself as one of the people

they want to reach. I often find I'd be offended by their stereotyping and condescending attitude.[7]

A Light to the Gentiles

After the infant Jesus was circumcised and the ceremonial period had been fulfilled, he was brought to the Temple in Jerusalem to be presented to the Lord. There he was met by a devout old man named Simeon, who blessed him and uttered a vision of the impact the baby in his arms would make as he ushered forth his Kingdom. Simeon said that Jesus would be "a light for revelation to the Gentiles" (Luke 2:32). This was a prophecy of the scandalous ways of Jesus because Gentiles were on the lowest rung of the social pecking order.

In the society of ancient Israel, there were five basic classes of people. First came the Pharisees, who were the religious elite, upstanding citizens and well versed in the law of Moses. Then came the common Jews, who were considered ignorant in their knowledge of the law. Next were the Galileans, a people of mixed blood who were considered inferior. They were just above the Samaritans, a race so despised that they had to build a temple of their own. And at the bottom of the heap were the Gentiles, whom the Jews called *dogs*. Each morning, every pious Jewish man would thank God he hadn't been born "a woman, a leper, or a Gentile." But it was to these very people—the lowest of the low—that Jesus continually reached out.

When Jesus publicly laid out his vision in the synagogue at Nazareth, the crowd initially loved what they heard:

The Spirit of the Lord is upon me,
  because he has anointed me
  to proclaim good news to the poor.
He has sent me to proclaim liberty to the captives
  and recovering of sight to the blind,
  to set at liberty those who are oppressed,
to proclaim the year of the Lord's favor.

LUKE 4:18-19

This all sounded good to the religious folks who had gathered for their weekly feeding from the Scriptures. As Luke notes about Jesus, "All spoke well of him and marveled at the gracious words that were coming from his mouth."[8]

Hear that? *Gracious words.* The congregation was thinking, *This is a really fine sermon. This young man's concepts and ideas are quite noble.* They thought Jesus was preaching rhetorically. But he actually meant what he said. He fully intended to carry out this mandate for ministry.

Keep in mind that Jesus was preaching to Pharisees and other pious Jews in his own hometown—the very same guys who gave thanks each morning that they were not Gentiles. And now Jesus is about to lose his audience. In fact, he is about to anger them to the point that they will try to murder him. What sets them off?

As Jesus continues his remarks, he brings up the fact that Elijah, the esteemed Old Testament prophet, had received relief from and worked a miracle for a widow in the Sidonian town of Zarephath, during a time of famine. And here's the rub. Although there were plenty of widows in Israel, Jesus says, Elijah did not go to any of them. Instead, he went to the home of a Gentile. Not only that, but Elijah's protégé, Elisha, chose to heal a Syrian leper, named Naaman, instead of healing one of the many lepers in Israel.

Why does Jesus point this out? To reveal the heart of God toward the Gentiles, the outcasts, and the downtrodden— and even toward the enemy, in the case of Naaman, a Syrian army commander. Jesus hacks away at the religious attitudes of the Jews in one fell swoop. He throws their sectarian prayers back in their faces.

"So you're glad you're not a woman, a leper, or a Gentile?" Jesus says in effect. "Well, a long time ago, through two of the greatest and most esteemed prophets of Israel, God showed his compassion on all three of those classes of society."

From the very outset, Jesus' ministry was to those whom the religious folks despised. Three particular classes of people received the lion's share of his attention: publicans (riffraff tax collectors), sinners (immoral individuals), and Gentiles (the lowest class). Matthew records that when Jesus left Nazareth, he "went and lived" in Galilee of the Gentiles.[9] He didn't just *visit* these people, he *dwelt* with them.

Holy How?

Many Christians, it seems, have adopted the perspective that it is impossible, or even compromising, to "love others as we love ourselves" when those *others* are living in what we believe is sin. How quickly we've forgotten our own sorry state of affairs when Jesus gave his life for *us*:

> For one will scarcely die for a righteous person—
> though perhaps for a good person one would dare
> even to die—but God shows his love for us in that
> while we were still sinners, Christ died for us.
>
> ROMANS 5:7-8

Jesus didn't die for us because he knew we would one day "accept" him. He died for us not only *before* we turned to him, but regardless of whether or not we would *ever* turn to him.

Jesus got into trouble with the religious leaders of his day precisely *because* of his friendships with prostitutes, tax collectors, and others the scribes and Pharisees had labeled as sinners. There's no disputing that these people were indeed sinners. Jesus never debated that point. He didn't say, "No, you've got it wrong. Who are you to determine what sin is?" No. Instead, Jesus turned the tables on the scribes and Pharisees and pointed out *their* sin—because *we're all sinners*. When a woman was caught in the act of adultery, Jesus didn't minimize or redefine her sinful behavior. But neither did he condemn her. Instead he said, "Let him who is without sin among you be the first to throw a stone at her."[10]

Perhaps because we have read the Gospel narratives so many times, the impact of Jesus' friendships with unchurchy people has lost its effect on our sensibilities. We don't really believe Jesus was an actual *friend* to "those people." Sure, they came around him and he bumped into them from time to time. But surely he didn't really *like* them and enjoy their company. From our twenty-first-century evangelical perspective, we figure Jesus was probably just nice to them so he could get them to come to church. Or maybe he was looking for the right moment to pray the sinner's prayer with them. But I think the answer was much simpler than that. Jesus was called "the friend of sinners" because *he was their friend.*

Have you ever bought a car "as is"? This means you agreed to take the vehicle in its present condition, rather than making the purchase contingent on certain repairs or upgrades being made. Jesus bought into people on an *as is* basis. He gave his life to buy back (redeem) you and me *just as we were*, not as we should have been. He knows he can make the repairs and upgrades later.

Not long ago, a church in St. Louis drew the ire of its denominational brethren when it started a monthly event at a local pub. Theology at the Bottleworks began as an outreach idea from The Journey church to discuss issues—such as the economy or global warming—that are relevant to the current culture. But there were those who couldn't stomach the idea that Jesus would approve of, much less initiate, sending his representatives into a bar.

Not every Christian is called to a ministry such as this. On the other hand, some Christians *are*. Neither group should criticize the calling and convictions of the other.

The approach that Jesus took was the polar opposite of that of the Pharisees—the *separatists*. Jesus refused to keep a safe distance from "worldly" people. Much to the chagrin of the religious conservatives of his day, he thrust himself into the normal happenings of *secular* culture. Jesus didn't stick to the synagogues. He went to the streets. He spent considerable time where the people were—in their social spaces, at public events, and at their parties. If we truly want to be *Christlike*, we must adopt his methods and mind-set as our own. In *Untamed*, their book about "missional discipleship," Alan and Debra Hirsch write:

> Too many Christians "hang out" only with other Christians and in environments frequented by other Christians. If we are to follow Jesus, we need to make intentional choices to move out of our religious zones and be where the people are. It will require that we come into direct social contact with others and become a regular part of the natural rhythms of their community.[11]

The principle of *incarnation* means that Christ followers must draw close to those whom God desires to redeem. We cannot demonstrate Christlikeness while remaining at a distance relationally from the people we are called by God to serve. We need to rub shoulders and have frequent conversations in actual friendship with people in our neighborhoods and workplaces—not just our church friends. We need to incarnate the presence of Jesus in the culture we live in by sharing meals, entertainment, hobbies, and sporting events with non-Christian friends. This is crucial if we hope to make sense of the gospel and its impact in the lives of others.

> All this is from God, who through Christ reconciled us
> to himself and gave us the ministry of reconciliation.
>
> 2 CORINTHIANS 5:18

This is the pattern Jesus models for us. He was an authentic friend of sinners. That doesn't mean he approved of or participated in their sin or avarice. But he loved to be with them and accepted them as they were. The holiness that Jesus walked in didn't push sinners away. It drew people to him in droves. Compare Jesus' influence to the "holiness" of the Pharisees and other ruling religious leaders, that kept sinners at bay.

The word *holy* means "set apart." To the Pharisees, this meant setting themselves apart from everyone but their own kind. In fact, the word *Pharisee* means "separated." Their very identity was wrapped up in their dedication to distancing themselves from the sordid influences of the world. In their minds, the sins of others—*uncleanness*, as they called it—would defile them if they mingled with sinners. Jesus, on the other hand, viewed holiness as being set apart *in service to God* by living and advocating his idea and meaning of life.

The scribes and Pharisees believed that holiness and godliness required *separation from* corruption and sin. Jesus demonstrated that holiness meant being *separated unto* the service of others on behalf of his Father. This continually led him to a place of *inclusion*, through which he poured out the mercy and compassion of God on *everyone*, not the least of whom were the very ones labeled as *unclean* by the religious leaders.

I like what Franciscan priest Richard Rohr says about this subject:

> Those at the edge of any system and those excluded from any system ironically and invariably hold the secret for the conversion and wholeness of that very group. They always hold the feared, rejected, and denied parts of the group's soul. You see, therefore, why the church was meant to be that group that constantly went to the edges, to the "least of the brothers and sisters," and even to the enemy. Jesus was not just a theological genius, but he was also a psychological and sociological genius. *When any church defines itself by exclusion of anybody, it is always wrong.* It is avoiding its only vocation, which is to be the Christ. The only groups that Jesus seriously critiques are those who include themselves and exclude others from the always-given grace of God.
>
> Only as the People of God receive the stranger, the sinner, and the immigrant, those who don't play our game our way, do we discover not only the hidden, feared, and hated parts of our own souls, but the fullness of Jesus himself. We need them for our own conversion.

The Church is always converted when the outcasts are re-invited back into the temple. You see this in Jesus' commonly sending marginalized people that he has healed back into the village, back to their family, or back to the temple to "show themselves to the priests." It is not just for their re-inclusion and acceptance, but actually for the group itself to be renewed.[12]

If I sincerely desire to be *like* Jesus and to actually be a *practicing evangelical*—a Good News person—then I must ask myself how I am living this out in the world. I must examine myself: "Am I like Jesus . . . a friend of *sinners*?" If I claim that I am, then I should be able to name those friends by name. I should be able to recount the times when we've hung out, shared meals, and shared life together. I may believe homosexuality is a sin, but do I have any gay friends? Have I spent time with them, doing the things that friends do? If the answer is *yes*, then have I treated them as actual friends or merely as evangelistic projects? What about other people I consider to be sinful? How do I think about those I consider my enemies? What is my inner thought life and prayer life in regard to them?

Throughout history, the religious establishment has always avoided certain people. But Jesus was an authentic friend to those very people. Allegiance to Jesus and to the Kingdom of God frees us and empowers us to love the world with the goodness and kindness of heaven, without fear, mistrust, or anger. Too often, we "fight the good fight of faith" with finger-pointing, fearmongering, and judgmentalism.[13] But that's not the faith we were called to. You could say we were called to have a "food fight," battling the powers of darkness with the fruit of the Spirit—love, joy, peace, patience, kindness, goodness, faithfulness, gentleness, and self-control.

To follow Jesus is to follow him in relationship with those who have called him their friend. Revangelicals are those who are willing and eager to retrace their steps to make sure they haven't "passed over" the people and things that Jesus called *the more important things*. For these folks, the "gracious words" of Jesus have become generative words of transformation in their hearts, minds, and deeds, separating them not *away from* religious outcasts, but separating them unto and into redemptive friendships and relationships.

QUESTIONS FOR REFLECTION

1. Who are the people most often despised and criticized by evangelicals today?

2. Who in your life would call you their friend, even though the religious community would label them *sinners*?

3. What categories or classes of people have you passed over in your life? Does anyone in particular come to mind?

4. What has been your definition of *holiness* to this point in your journey? In what ways should it change?

5. What are some ways you can re-enter the "world" you have passed over and separated yourself from?

5
REPRESENT

*The Word became flesh and blood, and
moved into the neighborhood.*

JOHN 1:14, MSG

*When Jesus was asked to reduce everything in the Bible
into one command he said: Love God with everything
you have and love your neighbor as yourself. What if
he meant that we should love our actual neighbors?
You know, the people who live right next door.*

JAY PATHAK AND DAVE RUNYON,
THE ART OF NEIGHBORING

THE PROPER THEOLOGICAL term for the Son of God
becoming human is *incarnation,* which means "in the flesh."

The Word became flesh and dwelt among us, and we
have seen his glory, glory as of the only Son from the
Father, full of grace and truth.

JOHN 1:14

I love it that John calls Jesus *the Word.* He uses the term several times in the first chapter of his Gospel. This means we
need look no further than Jesus if we want to know God's

perspective on something. He is God's word on everything. Let's say we want to know how to treat an enemy. Look at Jesus. If we want to know what God thinks about people who are far from him, look at Jesus. What should our attitude be about taxes? Look at what Jesus said about it.

As "the Word made flesh," Jesus was a walking-around, daily demonstration of the love of God. He was the flesh-and-blood manifestation of everything God stands for—and everything he won't stand for. He is God's opinion and commandment about every aspect of life—in living color. The beauty of the Incarnation is not that God came to earth and set up an organization and a headquarters. It is so much more—and so much better—than that. The blessing is that he "moved into the neighborhood," to borrow Eugene Peterson's evocative phrase. God took up residence in our midst, and he lived, worked, and played in human form on the very streets and in the neighborhoods of the people he sought to reach. The Incarnation is not only a historic and perpetual blessing; it is also a model for all followers of Jesus. The Incarnation is a cue for us to imitate Jesus, who said, "As the Father has sent me, even so I am sending you."[1] We are to see ourselves as *sent* into a particular part of the world, just as God sent Jesus.

Surprisingly, I've found very few Christians who have been taught this. In the churches I grew up in—so-called Bible-believing, gospel-preaching churches—we were never taught that God had sent everyday believers into their specific neighborhoods, just as he sent Jesus into the village of

Nazareth. If anything, we were taught to withdraw from "the world."

To be *revangelicaled*, we must take a closer look at *how* and *to whom* Jesus was sent, and what relevance his life and example have for how we live our lives today. Author Michael Frost elaborates on the theme of following Christ's example, drawing from the book of Philippians:

> Christians must be prepared to go where Christ would go: to the poor, to the marginalized, to the places of suffering. They must be prepared to die to self in order to follow Jesus' radical lifestyle of self-giving and sacrifice. . . .
>
> Paul . . . tells us that our "attitude should be the same as that of Christ Jesus" (Philippians 2:5). We often assume . . . [this] commends to us Jesus' humility, which is clearly present in the text. But Jesus' humility is . . . expressed in his commitments to *identification* and *relinquishment*. First, to follow Jesus' example means that we should share his profoundly humble identification with sinful humankind (Philippians 2:7-8). . . . [And we] should be aware of his equally humble willingness to empty himself and make himself nothing for the sake of God's redemptive purposes. . . . To embrace an incarnational ministry, then, involves a willingness to relinquish our own desires and interests in the service of others.[2]

One of the most attractive aspects of the gospel is that it creates a *new kind of person*. It doesn't produce a self-righteous person or a self-rights person. It creates a *selfless* person. We don't need to change the gospel. We don't need a new message. What we need—what the world needs—is a new type of *messenger*.

When Jesus announced the availability of the reign of his heavenly Father, it wasn't a warning of impending doom to be avoided, but an invitation of incredible joy and freedom to be entered into. This was *good news* to the people who heard it. And for those who had "ears to hear"—the qualifier Jesus so often added—it was *great* news.

Despite what so many street preachers would have you believe, the proclamation of the gospel—the arrival of the Kingdom of God on earth—did not portend a divine smackdown for those who would not change their ways. Jesus' emphasis was not on hell, but on the Kingdom of Heaven. Repent (turn around) because the wide-open door to God's glorious presence is right behind you. It is within reach. You are going the wrong way; but as soon as you turn around, you will walk straight into it.

Growing up, many of us evangelicals were taught that the word *repent* referred to a "bad news first" scenario. The message was, "You are a dirty, rotten sinner who is about to split hell wide open." That notion is not found in the Gospels or the preaching of Jesus. Are we sinners? No doubt. Would we go to hell without Jesus? For sure. But that's not the prevailing message of Jesus in Matthew, Mark, Luke, or John. The gospel is entirely *Good News*. "Turn around! The Kingdom of Heaven is right behind you. Grab on to it!"

Think about the last time you witnessed a street preacher standing on a milk crate with a megaphone, yelling to the crowds to repent because they are headed for hell. Does this verse describe him?

> How beautiful upon the mountains
>   are the feet of him who brings good news,
> who publishes peace, who brings good news of
>   happiness,
>   who publishes salvation,
>   who says to Zion, "Your God reigns."
>
> ISAIAH 52:7

Messengers of the Kingdom of God not only *speak* the good words of God's reign, they also bring those words to life. That is the essence of incarnational living. As these messengers live out the social ethics of the Kingdom of God, self-interest and self-preservation fall to the wayside in deference to an ethic of "love your neighbor as you love yourself."

When the gospel comes to life in us, when we become the new type of messengers that God intends for us to be, *love*, *acceptance*, and *forgiveness* become more than mere catchphrases or high-sounding ideals. They burst onto the scene, palpable and alive. When the words of Jesus are *embodied* (i.e., become living flesh and blood) in the lives of his followers as they move about in the places where they live, work, eat, and play, the *presence* of Jesus in the world becomes visible.

Just look at Jessica Eaves, a full-time college student, wife, and mother of four from Oklahoma, who recently found herself in the national spotlight when her story was picked up by news and Internet sites.[3] While grocery shopping one day, Jessica discovered her wallet had been stolen, and she was sure she knew who had taken it. Approaching a man who had been behind her at one time in the aisle where she was shopping, she said, "I think you have something of mine. . . . Give me my wallet and I'll forgive you right now, and I'll even take you to the front and pay for your groceries." The man reached into his pocket and gave Jessica her wallet. He began to cry and repeatedly apologized, adding that he had become desperate. Jessica spent twenty-seven dollars on his groceries, which included milk, bread, bologna, crackers, soup, and cheese. As they were checking out the man asked, "Why are you doing this?" Jessica answered, "Jesus forgives me every single day." Looking back, Jessica reflected, "The last thing he said was, 'I'll never forget tonight. I'm broke, I have kids, I'm embarrassed, and I'm sorry.'" In an interview with CNN, Jessica said, "What I did that day should be the norm."

Adapt or Die

In recent years, several books have pointed to the turnoff that Christianity has become for so many people. My friend Dan Kimball wrote *They Like Jesus but Not the Church,* a project that began not long after his encounter with a twentysomething gym instructor who found it hard to believe Dan was a pastor. She couldn't reconcile his mild-mannered persona, a keen familiarity with current punk rock bands, and his signature rockabilly hairstyle with her idea of what a pastor should be like. With emphasis, she said he could not possibly be a pastor because "Pastors are creepy." From her perspective, pastors "try to proselytize people to become right-wing Republicans," and "they hate homosexuals."[4]

Around the same time *They Like Jesus* hit the market, so did a book titled *unChristian*, by David Kinnaman and Gabe Lyons. Kinnaman and Lyons touch on many of the same themes Dan Kimball called attention to. Pointing to their own extensive research, they found that non-church-goers viewed Christians as insensitive to others, out of touch with reality, judgmental, and unChristlike—thus the name of their book.

Another book, which carries the provocative title of *Lord, Save Us from Your Followers*, highlights the culture-war battlefield that has come to personify Christianity in the eyes of many non-Christians—and a battlefield on which many evangelicals are convinced it is their duty to engage.

Some Christians acknowledge the negative public perception of evangelicals, but dismiss it as a persecutional badge of honor. It's simply the price of "standing for the truth," they say. Or it's further proof that "the darkness hates the light." No doubt there is some truth to these statements.

Jesus warned us in no uncertain terms that persecution would come. And now we are witnessing this come to pass.

For example, antitheist Richard Dawkins has called upon his fellow unbelievers to mock and ridicule religious people.[5] Atheist "churches" are springing up across America. And Christians are frequently made fun of and derided for their views on creationism and homosexuality, among other issues.

However, too often the problem is not the darkness hating the light. It's that the genuine kindness and goodness of the gospel light has been turned off or covered up.

Many evangelicals have scant awareness of the way we are viewed by the surrounding society. I've had more than one Christian friend become extremely defensive when I brought up the issue of the negative outlook that so many non-Christians have of evangelicals. Many Christians spend so much of their energy and focus on church-related activities and issues that they have no genuine friendships with non-Christians, other than people they work with, and almost all of their friends are fellow evangelicals. (My hunch is they don't have any actual non-evangelical friends.) Therefore, they have little idea of how evangelicals are viewed by the watching world, much less *why* we are viewed that way.

About twenty years ago, church leaders across America began to respond to dwindling church growth and attendance by rallying around the concept of *relevance*. The idea was that church had become too dull and boring, and this was surely why it had lost its appeal to outsiders. Church had become an out-of-touch turnoff for irreligious people.

Pastors and church leaders responded by overhauling music styles, redesigning church buildings, offering options for church service times, and serving up sermons focused on practical living. "This is not your grandma's church" became a common marketing angle. The basic idea was to prove that the church *can* relate with the current times and not be so outdated. And the hope was that if churches could change their image, people would respond. Aiming to alter *methods* without polluting the *message*, this shift became known as "the seeker movement."

The church's attempt at relevance calls to mind the old StarKist Tuna commercials, featuring Charlie the Tuna. Charlie was constantly trying to demonstrate how much style and class he had, in hopes of getting the attention of the StarKist folks. In one commercial, he might show up driving a high-end luxury touring car. In another, he would be wearing a smoking jacket and holding a martini. Charlie wanted everyone to know he had *good taste*. But he misunderstood what StarKist wanted. Every commercial ended with a fishhook dropping into the frame with a sign attached that read, "Sorry, Charlie," while the announcer declared, "StarKist doesn't want tuna with good taste. StarKist wants tuna that *tastes good*."

Two decades into the relevance trend, the decline in church growth continues—but even more rapidly. We have more megachurches than ever, bigger and cooler buildings and amenities, sermons bathed in theatrics, scenery, and set design, but the overall number of people attending church in America is the lowest in US history (by percentage of population).

There's something more than an image problem going on here. People aren't looking for churches with good taste.

They're looking for something that *tastes good*—as in "Taste and see that the LORD is good!" (Psalm 34:8). They're looking for *Good News people*—people with news they can't get from anyone else but Jesus. In the meantime, they're dropping a sign that says, "Sorry, church."

Recent reports have confirmed the hunches of these authors I've mentioned, and many others. The church in America is in big trouble. We're on the endangered species list. As evangelicals, we should be alarmed about our future prospects as a movement, as carriers of hope to a dying world.

Near the end of 2012, the Pew Forum on Religion and Public Life released an extensive report titled "'Nones' on the Rise." The research revealed that one-third (32 percent) of adults under the age of thirty have "no religious affiliation," compared with just one in ten (9 percent) who are sixty-five or older. "And young adults today are much more likely to be unaffiliated than previous generations were at a similar stage in their lives."[6] The research paints a bleak future. Canaries are dying in the coal mines.

Missiologist Alan Hirsch is a native of South Africa and has spent most of his adult life in Australia. Quite often, when he addresses a North American audience, he begins his talk by saying, "I come from your future." Alan explains that he has witnessed firsthand the decline of evangelical Christianity in a Western nation. Across Europe, huge cathedrals and church buildings host tiny congregations or have been turned into taverns and pubs. Evangelicalism is on life support there. These are warning signs of what happens when God's people lose touch with the people they are called to reach. If we don't wake up soon here in America, we will be in the same place as the European church before we know it.

Revangelicals are now responding to the call. Not a call to abandon the tenets of the Christian faith in order to cozy up to the culture. Far from it. The point is not how to compromise or adjust our beliefs so we can become relevant and appetizing for a twenty-first-century audience. The church has already tried that for more than two decades. This is a call to *return* to something—or more accurately, to *someone*. We must find our way back to the message and meaning of Jesus and the gospel (the *Good News*) he lived and preached. Nothing less will suffice. (That's the warning.) But nothing more is necessary. (That's the encouragement.)

The burden here is not to "return America to its roots." This is not a plea to bring back Ward and June Cleaver or Ozzie and Harriet Nelson. No. We must go back much further than that—two thousand years further. Evangelicals need a return to the roots of what caused observers to call the first followers of Jesus "little Christs" (the original meaning of *Christian*). People in the early church were called *Christians* because they were so Christlike. They stood out. They seemed like little versions of Jesus.

There Goes the Neighborhood

Everyone has a story of how they ended up in their neighborhood or apartment complex. Maybe you can point to a certain circumstance that brought you to the place where you now live, or maybe it seems like happenstance. But what matters more than how you got to where you are is what you're going to do now that you're there. How are you going to be a Good News person right there in your neighborhood?

We're so accustomed to being *consumers* that the concept of consciously and practically *investing* our lives into our cities and neighborhoods escapes us. For myself, I have found Jeremiah 29:4-7 to be one of the more heart-stirring passages of Scripture in this regard:

> Thus says the LORD of hosts, the God of Israel,
> to all the exiles whom I have sent into exile from
> Jerusalem to Babylon: Build houses and live in them;
> plant gardens and eat their produce. Take wives and
> have sons and daughters; take wives for your sons,
> and give your daughters in marriage, that they may
> bear sons and daughters; multiply there, and do not
> decrease. But seek the welfare of the city where I
> have sent you into exile, and pray to the LORD on its
> behalf, for in its welfare you will find your welfare.

This passage is full of the vitality and color of life. The Lord tells his people to enjoy life. He says to build homes and grow families and acquire the necessities of life. And then, in the final sentence, God adds something extremely important. He says to look out for the welfare of the cities *where he has sent us*. By using the word *sent*, the Lord makes it abundantly clear that we don't merely *live* in a particular place. We have been sent there—on purpose. And our purpose is to *seek the best* for our neighborhoods, communities, cities, and towns.

There's no mandate here to circle the wagons in a holy huddle. No, these are words of engagement, involvement, and investment.

With that in mind, when my wife and I became empty nesters about four years ago, we moved into a cozy house in the historic heart of Kansas City, Missouri. The Brookside area is one of those picturesque places with tree-lined streets, sidewalks, and shaded front porches, nourished by quaint coffee shops, homespun businesses, and neighborhood pubs. It is what is often referred to as a *walkable* neighborhood. I had always wanted to experience life in a neighborhood like this.

A couple of months after we moved in, a young couple, Jon and Alissa Shirley, purchased the home next to ours. Within five minutes of meeting Jon, he and I discovered we were both native Texans, and we also had several mutual friends across the country in ministry circles. We had been reading the same books and attending the same events, and we were both seeking to live our lives as *sent ones* from Jesus. Jon was a leader in a local church, and we were both working to navigate many of the same theological streams in an ever-changing church climate.

Meeting each other was an incredibly validating moment for both of us—and for our wives as well. We all felt it was confirmation that the Lord had indeed sent us to the Brookside neighborhood—not merely to occupy space on our street, but to actively seek to become a blessing to our neighbors.

Across the street from us, in a 1920s bungalow, we met an early-thirtysomething couple, Matt and Hilary, and their two little girls. If they had been part of the fictional scenario I created at the beginning of chapter 1, their reaction to the news that two evangelical families had moved into the neighborhood would not have been, "*Yes!* That's *great* news." In fact, we later learned that when another neighbor told Hilary that Jon and I were both "preachers," she said to Matt, "We've got to move! They are going to ruin the neighborhood!" When Matt didn't immediately respond, she added, "I'm serious, we've got to get out of here!"

Hilary is a flaming redhead who expresses her liberal social and political views with a torrid passion that matches the color of her hair. She will be the first to tell you that she loves old hymns, black church worship, and what Jesus is all about. But she's equally comfortable sharing her disdain for evangelical Christians and feels the world would be a better place without them.

Matt grew up in a Southern Baptist church, seldom missed a Sunday service during his childhood and teen years, and even had a collection of early Christian rock music on cassette tapes. Despite his heritage, he views the evangelical church in much the same way his wife does. As soon as he was old enough to leave home, Matt left the church, never to return. He calls himself an atheist, though I have my doubts about that.

Within a few months, Matt and Hilary placed their house on the market and very quickly received multiple offers.

Jon and Alissa and Sherri and I were sad they were going to be moving because something that Hilary would have never expected had begun to take shape: a *friendship*. We had all come to love Matt and Hilary, and they were a lot of fun to be around. And they seemed to genuinely like us in return. A few get-togethers over a meal, dessert, or drinks had cultivated a growing relationship. And because Jon and Alissa shared a similar life stage as parents of small children, they had become especially close with Matt and Hilary.

One afternoon, I was sitting on my front porch and noticed the For Sale sign was gone from their front yard. About that same time, Jon stepped outside to carry his recycling bins to the curb.

"So I guess Matt and Hilary will be moving soon," I said, nodding toward their house. "Man, I hate to see that."

Jon became animated as he said, "No, no, no, man! I was gonna tell you. They turned down all the offers and took the house off the market. Matt told me they couldn't bear to leave their old friends here—and us as well. They knew they would have to start off making new friends in a new neighborhood, and they decided they would miss us all too much."

"Imagine that," I said to Jon, laughing. "Hilary doesn't want to leave the evangelicals."

One evening, the six of us were sharing the bounty from my mother's homemade chocolate ice cream recipe, cranked out in the same freezer I had churned during my childhood.

As the conversation settled on the topic of Christianity and its current manifestation, I asked Matt what he thought it would look like if Jesus were to move into our neighborhood. He smiled and said, "I think we've already seen that. It would look like you guys."

So, what have we done that is so outstanding that Matt would respond to my question that way? Honestly, I don't know. There's nothing I could point to that goes beyond normal living. My only thought is that we've demonstrated an agendaless Christianity to Matt and Hilary. They're not evangelism projects for us, and I believe they can feel that. They're our friends.

As one of my personal spiritual disciplines, most mornings I pray for all the neighbors on our street by name, asking God to provide for their welfare in all aspects of life and that his Kingdom would come and his will would be done in their lives.

In the time we have lived in our neighborhood, I have gradually gotten to know more and more of our neighbors and more details of their lives. That helps me to pray more specifically for them, but I don't see them as evangelistic trophies to be won. They're my neighbors, and my friends.

Because Jon, Alissa, Sherri, and I have been open about who we are and have not had an agenda with our neighbors—other than to love them as we love ourselves—we can all talk very openly about our beliefs about God, politics, and everything else. We've had some great conversations in the neighborhood, with plenty of animation but without tension or anything close to anger. In fact, because of the tenor of our relationships, we are able to talk deeply about Jesus and his agenda for the world. Jon, Alissa, Sherri, and I have accepted and treated Matt and Hilary as friends, and they have responded in kind. We all thoroughly enjoy one another's company.

In Colossians 4:5-6, Paul instructs us about our relationships:

> Walk in wisdom toward outsiders, making the best use of the time. Let your speech always be gracious, seasoned with salt, so that you may know how you ought to answer each person.

For many evangelicals in the public square, their conversations and social media posts with those outside of Christianity are far from gracious and seasoned with salt. Quite often, their words are combative and condemning—seasoned with pepper and sour grapes. This is the opposite of walking in wisdom—which means it's *foolish*.

Far too often, I find myself with my head in my hands after watching yet another clip of a famous evangelical leader giving his opinion on a current issue or situation in the national news. The lack of grace so often demonstrated is just another log on the fire of vitriol toward evangelical Christianity, confirming our reputation as a bigoted, judgmental, misogynistic group of people.

Called to Serve

We've been taught that our most important aim with people outside the church is to "present the gospel." That typically means we offer them a set of facts or spiritual laws, culminating in an appeal to "accept Jesus Christ as their Lord and Savior." But what we've too often missed is that our *lives* are supposed to be a steady presentation of the gospel, whether we "evangelize" or not. By devoting our time, talents, and treasures to the service of God and allowing him to speak through our lives to the people we live among, we *are* presenting the Good News of God's Kingdom. The gospel isn't fish bait. It's fish *food*. When followers of Jesus *live out* the ways of the gospel, it opens doors (and ears) for the words of the gospel.

One of the best things about eating at a good restaurant is trying out the appetizers. Served in small portions, appetizers are not intended to fill us up. They serve a dual purpose: to take the edge off our hunger and tease it at the same time. Italian cuisine calls it *antipasto*, which means "before the meal." Think of the word *anticipate*. A good appetizer causes us to eagerly *anticipate* the full meal. That's how our lives should be to the people around us. In a sense, we should be *appetizers of heaven*.

Christians who live with a gospel intention in their lives become a sign of what is to come. They become a foretaste of heaven, making God's grace and kindness available through their redemptive living.

Let me tell you why you are here. You're here to be
salt-seasoning that brings out the God-flavors of
this earth.

MATTHEW 5:13, MSG

From a practical standpoint, it doesn't take a lot to make a big
difference. Jon Shirley and I decided that one way we could
live redemptively was by pooling our resources on lawn tools.
We share a lawn mower, snowblower, weed whacker, and leaf
blower. We go in together on fuel and maintenance costs,
and we also use our lawn tools to help out other neighbors.
For instance, it makes no sense for everyone on the block
to own a snowblower. Living redemptively means that the
handful of times it snows each winter in Kansas City, Jon and
I clear Matt and Hilary's driveway, as well the driveway of
the single lady who lives on the other side of Jon and Alissa.
It's no big deal. It doesn't have to be a huge thing to make
an impact.

Because we're part of a culture that is addicted to the
spectacular, the big splash, we can often overlook and fail
to do the simple, small, needful things for others. But those
little things can make a big difference. Let's remember how
Jesus defined greatness:

You know that the rulers of the Gentiles lord it over
them, and their great ones exercise authority over
them. It shall not be so among you. But whoever
would be great among you must be your servant, and

whoever would be first among you must be your slave, even as the Son of Man came not to be served but to serve, and to give his life as a ransom for many.

MATTHEW 20:25-28

Jesus tells us to stop trying to be noticed; to stop trying to be out front. He said the great ones are those who pick up the mantle of a servant. Think about that. What does your apartment complex or neighborhood look like from a servant's perspective? If you were to adopt the posture of a servant, how differently would you view your neighbors, and what else would you see around you that you've been "passing over" for years?

For more than thirty years, I have been engaged in what most Christians call *the ministry*. But the word has lost its original meaning. When people speak of "the ministry," they typically mean a paid professional career path. But the word *minister* simply means "to serve," and *ministry* simply means "service." I can't count the times that men and women have said to me, "I hope to be in the ministry someday." Or, "I just wish God would give me a ministry."

We must recover the meaning of *ministry*. No one can stop anyone from "being in the ministry." All you have to do is find a way to serve other people, and you're *in the ministry*. It's past time that we free the gospel of the Kingdom of God from its false prison of platitudes and church buildings. No one can stop you from serving, and there is no shortage of places or people to serve. You're not waiting to "go into the ministry." Your ministry is waiting for you to start serving.

Following Jesus into his Kingdom means we allow him to heal the blindness that causes us to view the world from a shallow, self-centered perspective. We must stop resisting him as he works to disengage us from the false values of status, power, and being on top. If we'll let him, he'll free us from our obsession with safety and security, and from our tendency to recoil from people on the fringes of society. Jesus invites us to fellowship with his marginalized friends, the ones he calls *lost* and the religious establishment calls *sinners*. Jesus invites us—you and me—to be *re-evangelized* by the Good News of his Father's Kingdom, which is characterized not by exclusiveness, fearful retreat, or defensive posturing, but by *in*clusiveness, engagement, and welcoming meals at the tables of sinners and saints.

Won't You Be My Neighbor?

One of the most familiar stories in the Gospels begins when a religious scholar makes the mistake of testing Jesus by asking him what would be necessary to obtain eternal life. As Jesus so frequently did, he turns the question back on the scholar, asking, "What is written in the Law? How do you read it?" The expert answered, "You shall love the Lord your God with all your heart and with all your soul and with all your strength and with all your mind, and your neighbor as yourself."[7]

Jesus told the scholar he had given a good answer and that he would *live* if he carried it out.

But the scholar had not yet reached his goal. "Looking for a loophole, he asked, 'And just how would you define "neighbor"?'"[8]

Now, before you climb onto your self-righteous high horse and judge the religious scholar, ask yourself the same question. How would *you* define "neighbor"?

Let's forget about what the word *neighbor* means in the original Greek text of the New Testament, as if there's a nuanced interpretation that might get us off the hook, and let's just cut to the chase. We're all familiar with the parable of the Good Samaritan (or we can quickly familiarize ourselves by reading Luke 10:25-37), so let's get straight to the bottom line: Which of the three travelers "proved to be a neighbor to the man who fell among the robbers?"[9]

"The one who treated him kindly."[10]

"Go and do the same."[11]

For Jesus (and as his followers, for us), the question is never, "Who is my neighbor?" The question is always, "Who will *be a neighbor* in my name?"

Jesus doesn't want us to focus on what people *are* or *are not*. He wants us to focus on who he has made us to be: *agents of the Good News of the Kingdom of Heaven* (aka revangelicals).

QUESTIONS FOR REFLECTION

1. What would your community look like if numerous followers of Jesus were to "go and do the same" as Jesus did when he walked on this earth?

2. In what ways have you participated in the Word (Jesus) becoming flesh in your neighborhood? What other opportunities do you see?

3. Do you see yourself and your family as *sent servants* to your community? What does that look like in practical terms?

4. How would your thoughts and actions differ if you viewed yourself as a servant to your neighbors?

5. Are you willing to consistently pray for the welfare of your neighbors and for the Kingdom of Heaven to come and for God's will to be done for them?

6. What are some practical ways you can be a *Good News* neighbor and love your neighbors as you love your own life?

6
RENEW

Love applied to economics is Jubilee.

MARK VAN STEENWYK, *THE UNKINGDOM OF GOD*

GO BACK in your mind to January 20, 2009, the day Barack Obama was sworn in as the forty-fourth president of the United States of America. Now imagine that after the new president delivers his opening remarks, he hits the high notes of his inaugural address with the following statement:

My fellow Americans, on this day, we come to proclaim good news to the poor, freedom for prisoners, relief for the blind and the oppressed and for those who have been taken advantage of. The time has come to affirm that everyone who has been exploited or kept down by an unjust system will receive liberty from their repression.

Oh, and one more thing . . . I hereby declare 2009 to be a Year of Jubilee. This means all debts are canceled and everyone whose home has been foreclosed on will get their homes back. Everyone gets a fresh start . . .

If an American president were to announce such an agenda, he would at once be the most loved and most reviled man on the face of the earth. His message would represent hope for some, but a threat to others. Those at the bottom of the social heap would sing his praises; those at the top would likely seek every means at their disposal to undermine his message, agenda, and reputation—or worse. His very life might be in danger. Enemies would quickly emerge from both the political and financial power centers of our nation, seeking to preserve the status quo.

Such was the case when Jesus first came on the scene in ancient Israel. He threatened both the religious and political power grids with some crazy ideas about justice, peace, and forgiveness. It wasn't his view of God that got him killed. It was his view of the world. It's the same worldview that is often ignored today by many people who claim to live *in Jesus' name.*

The Spirit of the LORD is upon Me,
Because He has anointed Me
To preach the gospel to the poor;
He has sent Me to heal the brokenhearted,

To proclaim liberty to the captives
And recovery of sight to the blind,
To set at liberty those who are oppressed;
To proclaim the acceptable year of the LORD.

LUKE 4:18-19, NKJV

This was Jesus' inaugural speech, delivered not on the steps of the Capitol, but at the synagogue in his hometown of Nazareth. This was how he presented the platform for his administration as King of kings and Lord of lords. He was saying, "This is why I came. And here's what we're going to do . . ."

And wow! This was radical stuff. It sounded just as revolutionary to the people present on that day two thousand years ago as it would today if an American president were to make the same proclamation.

But was this just a speech to stir up a crowd, or did Jesus actually intend to carry out such an extreme agenda?

Jesus introduced a new social order. He not only proposed it; he lived it. But he didn't try to do it alone. From the start, he recruited others to join him in his revolution.

When he began their orientation, he might as well have said, "Everything you've heard up to this point in your life is wrong," because he proceeded to turn their thinking upside down. The changes Jesus brought were nothing short of a social revolution. *Check your selfishness and upward mobility at the door. Transform your independence into interdependence. There's no room for self-serving individualism in this administration.*

Jesus said he came "to proclaim the year of the Lord's favor."[1] Scholars agree this is a clear and direct reference to the Year of Jubilee, as described in Leviticus 25:10:

> You shall consecrate the fiftieth year, and proclaim
> liberty throughout the land to all its inhabitants.
> It shall be a jubilee for you, when each of you shall
> return to his property and each of you shall return to
> his clan.

God had decreed that every fifty years, all slaves were to be released and all land returned to its original owners. This meant the land went back to *everyone*, because it had originally been given to everyone. This periodic redistribution was God's way of keeping capital assets from aggregating in the hands of the few. E. Stanley Jones explains the idea behind Jubilee:

> The Year of Jubilee was intended to right the
> relationships between man and man, and man
> and the land, and man and money. It was all in
> the direction of an approximate equality. It kept
> individuals from accumulating from generation to
> generation and thus gaining control over others
> by economic means. A brotherhood could only
> be produced and maintained as gulfs between the
> individuals were not allowed to form and widen
> because of economic inequality. The Year of Jubilee

was intended to bring men back to equality and
hence to brotherhood.[2]

Let's look at the growing disparity between rich and poor in
the United States, which is at an all-time high. A living wage
is now out of reach for millions of Americans, while corporate chiefs continue to pocket more and more income. Try
living on a salary of $15,080 a year. That's the annual gross
income of a person who works full time at minimum wage.
Try to find a place where you can afford an average two-
bedroom apartment on that income. There is no such place.
In fact, in a lot of cities, you could work 24/7 (168 hours
a week) and still not be able to pay the rent, let alone buy
anything else, such as food, clothing, etc.

If adjusted relative to inflation, the minimum wage today
would be at least $10.67 an hour, rather than $7.25—and
even that adds up to only $22,194 per year, which is well
below the wage of $34,645 earned by the average American
worker. Now compare that to the average CEO compensation in the United States of $12,259,894.[3]

A *Los Angeles Times* article titled "CEO-to-Worker Pay Gap
Is Obscene; Want to Know How Obscene?" reports on a battle
between corporate America and the Securities and Exchange
Commission rule requiring companies to calculate the ratio
of their CEO's pay to the median pay of all their employees:

It's also not a new finding that outsized CEO
compensation depresses employee morale, especially

among middle managers. The great management guru Peter Drucker advised companies to stick to a ratio of about 20 to 1 between the pay of the CEO and that of the average worker. That's "the limit beyond which they cannot go if they don't want resentment and falling morale to hit their companies," Drucker wrote. . . .

Drucker's standard was in line with the ratios of the 1970s and early '80s, when he wrote those words. Today they seem positively quaint. The average CEO-to-worker pay ratio in 2012 was about 350 to 1. That's down somewhat from where it was before the 2008 recession, but it would have to come down a great deal more to return to the non-obscene range.[4]

Oppressing workers is something the Lord strictly forbids and detests (Isaiah 58:3). With close to two million workers in the US making minimum wage, why is this not one of the hot-button sins that today's evangelicals harp on?

Likewise, how is it possible that Sunday after Sunday, professing Christians sit together on the same pews, partake together of Communion (which, by the way, means "common union"), sing worship songs about giving their total devotion to Jesus, and then exit the building to live their *real* lives in consumptive individualism?

How can we call this Christianity when one family leaves the church parking lot in a $50,000 SUV to feast at a fine restaurant and return to an enormous, palatial home, while the single mom walking out behind them loads her children into a smoke-puffing beater of a car and drives home to an apartment or house where she will go to bed worrying about how she can afford to feed her kids that week or whether the electricity will be cut off before her next paycheck?

The spirit of Jubilee gets to the very essence and substance of the reign of God on earth. It is a core principle of the gospel of the Kingdom of Heaven. God, in his brilliant wisdom, kindness, and goodness, has provided more than enough for everyone on earth to live. But when greed and excess create mountains of inequality, valleys of need and despair evolve.

That's why the Lord sends his Good News people, in the spirit of Jubilee, to make up the difference.

Roger and Marianne are young church planters in Kansas City. They are also revangelicals. Just a few months after they started their life together as a married couple, a young man named Brendon, who had been disowned by his father and unjustly imprisoned, came out of the penal system with no place to go. At night, he was sleeping wherever he could find a place—on friends' couches, park benches, or in someone's car.

When Roger and Marianne heard about Brendon's situation, they invited him to come live with them.

Now, nothing could be more inconvenient and intrusive for a young couple in the early stages of marriage than to add a third person to an apartment with less than seven hundred square feet of living space, but Roger told me that he and

Marianne felt that the gospel of the Kingdom called them to share their abundance. And even though their place was tiny, they had a spare bedroom.

In the time Brendon has been with them, he has come to faith in Christ and has become a treasured member of their church community.

One of the primary themes of the Kingdom gospel is *conversion*. To "repent and believe in the gospel" (Mark 1:15) means to change one's viewpoint and to follow up with actions that flow from a new way of seeing the world.

Evangelistic reductionism has shriveled the meaning of "repent and believe" to something like this: "You are headed for hell when you die unless you stop and ask God to forgive your sins." That interpretation falls woefully short of the message of Jesus, which was and still is, "The ways of the world are selfish, harmful, and wrong. Turn around and pursue the Kingdom of Heaven instead."

That doesn't mean we're to set our sights and our hopes on a someday celestial realm with pearly gates, streets of gold, and cotton candy clouds, all within earshot of a 24/7 worship service. The in-breaking Kingdom of God is nothing if not personal, practical, and immediate.

The conversion that Jesus spoke of is not merely an *adjustment* to our usual lifestyle. To repent and believe means to *turn around* and follow the ways and means of heaven. It really is a change in worldview; that is, the way we view other people—dirty people, trashy people, mean people, enemy people, and inconvenient people. It is a change in the way we view our possessions—how we hold on, how we lend, how we share. It is a change in our loyalties—to family, God, and country. Jesus challenges us on our *entire* lives. When we truly put him first, it changes *everything*.

The Foolishness of the Cross

Paul refers to the upside-down thinking of Jesus as the *folly* of the Cross (1 Corinthians 1:18). I imagine he laughed when he wrote that. I can also imagine the disciples on multiple occasions whispering to one another during one of Jesus' public talks: "He's *loooooosing* it."

We usually look at a cross as a means of death. But Jesus said it is the way to life:

> If any of you wants to be my follower, you must turn from your selfish ways, take up your cross daily, and follow me. If you try to hang on to your life, you will lose it. But if you give up your life for my sake, you will save it.
>
> LUKE 9:23-24, NLT

Jesus brought a new worldview and a new world order. It is called the gospel of the Kingdom of Heaven. The problem we have with the Kingdom is that it never "adds up." It never makes sense to our earthly minds. The Kingdom is incalculable. This inability to assure outcomes is one of the fundamental stumbling blocks; what Paul calls "foolishness to Gentiles" (1 Corinthians 1:23, NIV). This is why our walk with the Lord is *by faith*. We let go of demanding to be able to calculate our own safety and security.

I've found that capitalism can be a major stumbling block that keeps American evangelicals from entering into the ways of the Kingdom of Heaven. One sure way to stir a drowsy evangelical awake is to bring up the subjects of *socialism* and *capitalism*. Very quickly, both hands will grip the sides of his chair as he pushes up and readjusts to a proper defensive mode. (Be honest now; didn't your blood pressure move up a tick or two as you read this paragraph?)

Capitalism is based on a free market of open competition that offers profit and private ownership as motives for production and job creation. It favors individuals as it encourages private investment and business development. Capitalists have the freedom to own and use wealth to sell products or services, to hire workers and distribute profits, with little government control or interference. The beauty of capitalism is the opportunity it offers (in theory) for everyone to be able to play the game. The ugly side of capitalism is the temptation and opportunity for overarching greed that creates an ever-increasing divide between the *haves* and *have-nots*.

Socialism (in theory) emphasizes the benefit of the people at large. The spreading of the wealth for the common good is the stated ideal that undergirds this heavily governmentally involved system. Socialist governments divert money to public programs. The upside of socialism is the theory of "enough for everyone." The downside is the lack of freedom and incentive for innovation and production that a free market society provides. The methods of coercion and the will to power that characterize real-world communism and socialism inevitably undermine and circumvent the spirit of commonality.

The ways of the Kingdom are neither capitalist nor socialist. The Lord never uses oppression to beat oppression. He uses grace to dismantle ungrace. The gospel of the Kingdom of Heaven isn't predicated on theories of economics or political systems. It is based on a transformation of the heart that shows itself in compassionate and generous caring for our fellow human beings.

The cop-out from so many Christians is that they don't want to be *forced* to share with others; they prefer to *give freely* as the Lord would have them do. But if you've ever looked at studies of giving levels compared to income, it's pretty clear that most Christians who say they want to give freely don't, and most are not purveying a biblical lifestyle that aims for a "common good." These same folks are quick to scream, "Socialism!" whenever politicians speak in terms of the common good in relationship to taxes. So nothing significantly changes in our society.

Efforts at imposing a "return to our roots" in America usually revolve around narrow categories of so-called moral issues, such as prayer in schools, definitions of marriage, and what it means to be pro-life. We could learn a lot from revangelicals such as those in the group Evangelicals for Social Action (ESA), who publish scholarly books and articles, along with a weekly e-newsletter, to inform individual Christians and churches of the reality of the plight of the poor and oppressed and encourage Christ followers everywhere to work out the practice of the gospel of the Kingdom of Heaven.

ESA works on behalf of the oppressed and marginalized throughout the world to shed light on issues needing peace and justice. They describe themselves as "one of the only evangelical organizations that consistently campaigns at the grassroots and policy level for a world that is pro-life and pro-poor, pro-family and pro-racial justice, pro-sexual integrity, and pro-creation care."[5]

The gospel of the Kingdom of Heaven is not a new policy or competing ideology. It is not a system that is *imposed* on anyone. It is an *offer*. It flourishes only in an ethos of willingness. The gospel is not a political system, but make no mistake, it *is* an economic system. It is not a governmental system, but it is a social system. The gospel of the Kingdom of Heaven is God's idea of how human society should function on earth. And the spirit of Jubilee underpins that gospel message.

Our most common interpretation of the gospel as a message for *individuals* stems from our viewing it through the lens of capitalism—when all along Jesus intended to introduce the gospel of the Kingdom of Heaven as a new *social platform*. The Jubilee of the gospel is not only an *individual* awakening and rebirth, but it is meant to be a *collective* awakening and rebirth into a *familial* worldview. The economy of the Kingdom, by which the people of God are to operate, is not to be driven by capitalist, socialist, or communist paradigms. The platform would more fittingly be called Jesusism.

I find it frightening and appalling that millions of evangelical Christians tune in daily to talk shows hosted by politicos and economists who thump the Bible with ill-formed theological views that clearly run counter to the gospel of Jesus and his Kingdom. A straightforward reading of the Gospels leaves no justification for disqualifying *anyone* from kindness, compassion, mercy, and tangible help. At the same time, they leave no room for greedy, petty, prideful people who posture themselves as superior or somehow separate from others.

The bane of American evangelicalism is that we have filtered the words of Jesus through capitalistic and individualistic perspectives, policies, and positions. In effect, we've told Jesus he can't enter our kingdom with his irrational ideas. As E. Stanley Jones writes, "Christianity has been looked on as an impracticable thing which might work in heaven, but not on earth."[6]

The Acceptable Year of the Lord

The hope for this world lies in a new breed of evangelical—*revangelicals* who are filled with as much emotion and vigor for the ideas of the Kingdom of Heaven as they are for patriotism and capitalism. Jesusism is the only answer for a habitable and thriving social order.

> Jesus said to his disciples, "I tell you the truth, it is very hard for a rich person to enter the Kingdom of Heaven. I'll say it again—it is easier for a camel to go through the eye of a needle than for a rich person to enter the Kingdom of God!"
>
> MATTHEW 19:23-24, NLT

Most American evangelicals give scant notice to what Jesus says here because most do not consider themselves rich. The problem is, we measure ourselves against the upper crust of our own society and not against the rest of the world. The fact is, the average American is in the top 2 percent of the richest people on the planet. The camel-and-needle metaphor is Jesus' way of telling us, "You can't bring your ideas, ways, and human justifications into my Kingdom. If you want to follow me, you must unload!"

The Year of Jubilee was remarkable in its platform of freedom for slaves, restitution of property, and the closing of the economic gap. The spirit behind it was a brotherhood of mankind. It broke down walls of division. So when Jesus uses the metaphor of the Year of Jubilee as his administrative platform for his heavenly Kingdom *on earth,* he makes an enormous, world-changing proposal. And then he recruits his disciples with a simple invitation: "Follow me." He invites us to join him on that agenda.

Following Jesus always requires the abandonment of other agendas . . . even lifelong agendas. When Peter, James, and John accepted that invitation, they "dropped their nets" on the spot and left behind everything they knew and had worked for.[7] The same thing happened with the other disciples. But there were others that Jesus invited into his Jubilee agenda who could not stomach the requirements of abandoning lifelong paradigms and commitments.

> To another he said, "Follow me." But he said, "Lord, let me first go and bury my father." And Jesus said to him, "Leave the dead to bury their own dead. But as for you, go and proclaim the kingdom of God." Yet another said, "I will follow you, Lord, but let me first say farewell to those at my home." Jesus said to him, "No one who puts his hand to the plow and looks back is fit for the kingdom of God."
>
> LUKE 9:59-62

If you're like me, this passage seems unreasonable on Jesus' part. Don't attend your own father's funeral? Seriously? Don't tell your family good-bye and let them know where you're going? Jesus uses extreme examples here to jolt us into the all-encompassing enormity of what it means to follow him. In essence, he is grabbing us by the shoulders, squaring eyes with us, and saying, "If you want to follow me, you must follow *me*." As fully devoted followers of Jesus, we will not be able to go after the things we've been pursuing for our entire lives. Jesus underscores the commitment level required to join him, follow him, and enter into his Kingdom initiatives.

The early church took Jesus quite seriously. The spirit of

Jubilee took hold of their hearts and minds and manifested in a collective of people whose individualistic agendas were swept away in the tide of Jesusism.

> And all the believers met together in one place and shared everything they had. They sold their property and possessions and shared the money with those in need. They worshiped together at the Temple each day, met in homes for the Lord's Supper, and shared their meals with great joy and generosity—all the while praising God and enjoying the goodwill of all the people. And each day the Lord added to their fellowship those who were being saved.
>
> ACTS 2:44-47, NLT

> All the believers were united in heart and mind. And they felt that what they owned was not their own, so they shared everything they had. The apostles testified powerfully to the resurrection of the Lord Jesus, and God's great blessing was upon them all. There were no needy people among them, because those who owned land or houses would sell them and bring the money to the apostles to give to those in need.
>
> ACTS 4:32-35, NLT

Evangelical pastors and leaders have prayed and preached for decades in hopes of producing the type of results the early church witnessed, where thousands of people were converted and healed in short order. But have we, as congregations of evangelicals, bought in to the lifestyle of mutuality and authentic brotherhood of the early church—a lifestyle the early Christians considered *normal*—or have we approached Christianity on our own terms?

When Jesus sat in the synagogue on the day of his inaugural "Kingdom of Heaven" speech, he declared "the acceptable year of the Lord" (as some older English translations phrase it).[8] Many years ago, I heard an elderly preacher highlight that phrase, pointing out that this is what God considers acceptable.

I think the old preacher made a great point: God doesn't accept our terms. He demands and accepts only *his* ways and means of forming and ruling his Kingdom. We're mistaken if we believe God will approve of a form of Christianity that turns a blind eye to a lifestyle of hoarding and social upscaling while turning away from the very people in need in our midst.

The undeniable fact of the earliest response by followers of Jesus was that they lived under a gospel code that drove them to live for the common good. The summation of all that Jesus taught caused them to conclude that living one for all and all for one was what Jesus both proposed and demanded. Anything less was not the *acceptable* form of his Kingdom.

Kingdom Economy

When some evangelicals read accounts of the early church in Acts 2 and 4, their tendency is to dismiss the details as not applicable in our day and age—"It was different back then"—or to conflate scriptural principles of compassion and generosity with contemporary examples of communism or socialism, and thus dismiss them outright. But such attitudes are shortsighted, failing to recognize that Satan will always seek to pervert the things he wants to prevent. In order for a lie to be believed, it must look as close to the truth as possible. Communism and socialism (in their ideals) may seem to have traits that are consistent with what we find in these passages from Acts. But the ethic of the gospel of the Kingdom of Heaven is not communist or socialist. At the same time, the gospel *is* very much *communal* and *social*.

When truly entered into, the Kingdom of Heaven sows the seeds of the Word of God in people's hearts and minds. The effect is a new social value system. Selfish acquisition is melted down into collective well-being. In the Kingdom of Heaven, those who have more—whether it is more talent, treasure, skill, or education—steward it for the collective good and become rich in fellowship and brotherhood.

Cherith Brook

Cherith Brook is a community of Jesus followers who live their lives with and for people that our culture often dismiss as inconvenient and burdensome.

Following several years of traditional pastoral ministry, Jodi and Eric Garbison became increasingly burdened about the life of the church the other six days of the week. Jodi says they felt the church was "painfully silent on things that really matter." After living in an intentional community of believers in Atlanta for a couple of years, Jodi, Eric, and their children, Ana and Henri, returned to Kansas City, responding to a call to start a community. Feeling drawn to a location on a busy street in the urban corridor, the family moved into an apartment above an old commercial building. While their children were at school, Jodi and Eric found themselves spending most of each day developing relationships with the people who called the street their home.

Though the Garbisons are Presbyterians, they drew inspiration and insight from the Catholic Worker movement and the wisdom and experience of the late Dorothy Day. Jodi says, "The spirit of nonviolence, peacemaking, and permanent presence in the neighborhood formed our vision of what gospel living means. If you are feeding your neighbor, you can't be killing him. If you are gardening, you can't be killing the earth."[9]

Jodi and Eric discovered that one of the greatest unmet needs of the homeless in their area, besides food and clothing, was a place to take a shower. So they started there, making their shower available to people with whom they were developing friendships. Eight years later, Cherith Brook has become an oasis of refreshment for the needy. The Garbisons and a handful of others live in a historic home adjacent to the outreach headquarters. Several shower areas are now available, along with a well-stocked clothing exchange closet, from which those in need are able to get a fresh set of clothes on a regular basis. Each morning, a sit-down breakfast is offered in an inviting setting that looks like a little hometown diner, complete with tablecloths and bowls of fresh fruit on the tables.

The Cherith Brook community includes a thriving urban garden, with chickens, honey-producing bees, and bountifully producing fruit trees. The servant team that lives in the house practices intentional community. They share resources, including pooling their income from outside jobs, in a "common purse" that meets everyone's personal needs. Jodi told me, "This means nobody has a burden too big to carry on their own, and no one has nothing to do and no responsibilities."

Cherith Brook is truly a "city set on a hill" (Matthew 5:14), shining the light of Jesus into the surrounding community. These Jesus followers have taken his words seriously and seek to bring his pronounced liberty to the cultural captives and oppressed ones in their midst. These Christians came to a place where the fabric of society had become withered and tattered, and they have used the fabric of their lives to reweave *shalom*—the gospel of peace—on a daily basis as they bring God's comfort and joy to their neighborhood.

Revangelicals—like those at Cherith Brook—have turned their backs on individualism and the spirit of ownership and possessiveness when it comes to finances and the rhythms of daily life. Instead, they perceive their resources not as their own, but as the Lord's. They've chosen *stewardship* in its most basic (some might say *radical*) meaning, rather than *ownership*, with its inclination toward excessive personal indulgence.

Revangelicals have taken up the mantle of servanthood

and view their lives as a calling to participate in the Jubilee of Jesus. This means an all-out commitment to the collective good, an idea that rubs raw against our capitalist sensibilities, which are based more on free market principles than on fair market principles.

The spirit of Jubilee is meant to be the *character*, *attitude*, and *complexion* of the church; that is, there is enough for everyone when everyone is satisfied with enough. That means living simply and sensibly in regards to *stuff*. The Jubilee mind-set is to be "rich toward God," in accordance with what Jesus taught about the dangers of hoarding:

> And he said to them, "Take care, and be on your guard against all covetousness, for one's life does not consist in the abundance of his possessions." And he told them a parable, saying, "The land of a rich man produced plentifully, and he thought to himself, 'What shall I do, for I have nowhere to store my crops?' And he said, 'I will do this: I will tear down my barns and build larger ones, and there I will store all my grain and my goods. And I will say to my soul, "Soul, you have ample goods laid up for many years; relax, eat, drink, be merry."' But God said to him, 'Fool! This night your soul is required of you, and the things you have prepared, whose will they be?' So is the one who lays up treasure for himself and is not rich toward God."

LUKE 12:15-21

Nowadays, we watch television shows about hoarders, people who keep just about everything, to the point where their homes are completely filled and barely livable. We judge these people and say to ourselves, *Wow, I'm glad I'm not like that.* Oh really? We are a nation of hoarders. It's just that most of us pay someone else to host our hoarding—to the tune of more than $23 billion per year.[10] This, in a nation in which nearly 80 percent claim to be followers of Christ.[11]

Another significant metric of our consumptive indulgence can be found in the category of housing. Over the past two generations, Americans have been conditioned to believe they need bigger and bigger houses. Following World War II, the first Levittown subdivision homes had about 750 square feet of living space. By the time the 1960s rolled around, the typical American home was 1,100 square feet. And over the last forty years, home sizes have continued to grow until the average size is now 2,500 square feet. Compare this to the average-sized home in the United Kingdom, which is still about 750 square feet.[12]

Revangelicals are people who choose to live according to what they *need*, not based on what they can *afford*. When Joey Turner invited others to form a core group to join in starting a church in the Fairmount neighborhood of Fort Worth, a wealthy couple decided to sell their $800,000 home and move into one at about one-fourth the cost, in order to join in the journey of planting a faith community in an economically and racially diverse neighborhood.

Scott, the husband, is a banker, and when he tells potential clients where he lives, eyebrows are raised because people in Fort Worth know that Fairmount is not the most upscale of communities. Why would a "successful" banker live in that neighborhood? Did this guy run into financial problems of his own? This opens the door for Scott to share the story of his family's decision to change their lifestyle for the sake of living and giving among people who have less.

The Kingdom of God is established on the organizing principle of ordinary and extraordinary people voluntarily letting go of their inferiorities and superiorities to commit themselves to genuine fellowship . . . a genuine faith community. These are some of the revangelicals who seek to live out the Jubilee principle of Jesusism. Their hope is to manifest and enter into the joy of seeing Isaiah 58:12 come to pass:

> Some of you will rebuild the deserted ruins of your
> cities.
> Then you will be known as a rebuilder of walls
> and a restorer of homes.[13]

Revangelicals embrace the tangible agenda of Jesus, which is intended to affect every social order in every epoch of history. They accept Jesus' invitation to enter the Kingdom of Heaven by adapting his ways and means as he teaches a new way to be human in a broken world of haves and have-nots. Jesus' Jubilee agenda challenges our faith. It calls us to believe that the gospel of his Kingdom will work on earth, just as it does in heaven. This Jubilee is a call to *re-normalize* community and brotherhood, in the process becoming rich with the treasures of heaven.

QUESTIONS FOR REFLECTION

1. In what ways do the ideas of the Jubilee of the gospel and the "folly of the Cross" challenge you?
2. How does this chapter challenge your worldview in relation to your responsibility toward others in your faith community and the community at large?
3. What are some ways you can start practicing Jubilee living?
4. What are some short-term (entry-level) goals?
5. What are some long-term goals?

7
RESTORE

*Jesus puts two contrasts before us. He speaks of the broad
way and the narrow way. The broad way that many
are taking is the way of vicious cycles. The narrow
way is joyous participation in the reign of God.*

GLEN STASSEN

*Most people know that Jesus came to bring forgiveness
and grace. Less well known is the Biblical teaching that
a true experience of the grace of Jesus Christ inevitably
motivates a man or woman to seek justice in the world.*

TIM KELLER

*And what does the LORD require of you? To act justly
and to love mercy and to walk humbly with your God.*

MICAH 6:8, NIV

MY PARENTS tried to have children for the first ten years of
their marriage, but they were unable to conceive. Eventually,
they adopted my sister. Three years later—*surprise!*—my
mom was pregnant, with me.

Growing up, my sister and I had arguments from time
to time, like any two siblings, and as the younger brother, I
took my share of verbal lumps. Sibling warfare can be a tricky
business. Battles are won or lost based on stealth, speed,

cleverness, and wit. One day when I was about six years old, I made a huge tactical error in the trenches of mouth-to-mouth combat.

I had devised a plan I was certain would shut my sister up and give me the victory. She would learn a lesson that she would never forget, and she would think twice before tangling with me again. I was ready to pull it out, like a flash-bang grenade, and yank the pin at just the right moment the next time we had a full-blown fight.

Shock and awe.

It wasn't long before I got my chance.

One evening, in the midst of a barrage of barbs hurled back and forth at one another, I saw my opportunity. Lurching my neck forward, I fired my nuclear verbal missile right between her eyes.

"Adopted!"

This was a low blow for sure. What a cruel thing to say. Like a punch to the gut, I thought it would drop her to the mat, staggered, dazed, and confused. I was wrong.

It was as if my sister had been preparing for this moment for years. Like a prizefighter anticipating her opponent's sneaky left hook, she pulled her head back and watched the verbal blow sail harmlessly by.

Now *I* was confused. Maybe it was just taking a few seconds to sink in.

My sister stared at me. Silent.

Okay, here come the waterworks, I said to myself.

Wrong again.

"Let me tell you something, you little twerp," she said. Her eyes narrowed and her head tilted menacingly as she walked toward me. "Momma and Daddy *chose* me. They just got *stuck* with you."

With that, my sister smiled, turned, and walked out of the room. I had been KO'd.

Jesus was chosen. He was appointed by his heavenly Father for the task of bringing the Kingdom of God to earth, just as it is in heaven. And Jesus chose all his followers to join him in this heavenly work on earth.

When one of the teachers I had in grade school wanted the class's undivided attention, she would always say, "Put on your thinking caps." That's what I am asking you to do here. If we really want to get our heads and hearts around the teaching of the New Testament, we have to start with the background of the Old Testament. We can demonstrate this by looking at the baptism of Jesus in the context of Isaiah 42.

The Gospel accounts tell us that the Holy Spirit descended on Jesus like a dove and spoke these words: "This is my beloved Son, with whom I am well pleased."[1] The crowd of onlookers would have recognized this statement as the opening line of Isaiah 42—words so familiar that the rest of the passage might have echoed in their ears. It would be as if someone today were to sing the opening words of "Amazing Grace." In your mind, you would continue the phrase, "How sweet the sound, that saved a wretch like me." It's even possible that the entire song would play in your mind—and you might have it running in your head for the remainder of the day! So, when the crowd at the Jordan River heard, "This is my beloved Son, with whom I am well pleased," they knew exactly where the phrase originated, as well as the rest of the message:

> Behold my servant, whom I uphold,
>> my chosen, in whom my soul delights;
> I have put my Spirit upon him;
>> he will bring forth *justice* to the nations.
> He will not cry aloud or lift up his voice,
>> or make it heard in the street;
> a bruised reed he will not break,
>> and a faintly burning wick he will not quench;
>> he will faithfully bring forth *justice*.
> He will not grow faint or be discouraged
>> till he has established *justice* in the earth;
>> and the coastlands wait for his law.

ISAIAH 42:1-4 (italics added)

> God, the LORD, created the heavens and stretched them
>> out.
>> He created the earth and everything in it.
> He gives breath to everyone,
>> life to everyone who walks the earth.
> And it is he who says,
> "I, the Lord, have called you to demonstrate my
>> *righteousness*.
>> I will take you by the hand and guard you,

and I will give you to my people, Israel,
    as a symbol of my covenant with them.
And you will be a light to guide the nations.
    You will open the eyes of the blind.
You will free the captives from prison,
    releasing those who sit in dark dungeons.

ISAIAH 42:5-7, NLT (italics added)

Notice the usage of the words *justice* and *righteousness*:

"He will bring forth *justice* to the nations [peoples]."

"He will faithfully bring forth *justice*."

"He will not grow faint or be discouraged till he has
established *justice* in the earth."

"I, the LORD, have called you to demonstrate my
righteousness."

One of my favorite bookshelf treasures is an old copy of the
Oxford Universal Dictionary. My edition, which is about five
inches thick and weighs around twenty pounds, was printed
in 1955. This great old dictionary often includes in its definitions the evolution of a particular word. Sometimes it's surprising, even shocking, to see how a word means something
completely different today than it did maybe a hundred years
ago. The word *righteousness* is a word like that.

In the fourth Beatitude, Jesus says, "Blessed are those who hunger and thirst for righteousness, for they shall be filled" (Matthew 5:6, NKJV). Righteousness has come to be understood by most evangelicals as being in good standing (that is, being right) with God. But this is where our English understanding of the word fails us—and it's crucial that we don't miss the biblical meaning of the word *righteousness*. Professors Glen Stassen and David Gushee offer some help:

> What are we hungering and thirsting after when we hope and long for righteousness? . . .
>
> Because our culture is individualistic, we think of righteousness as the virtue of an individual person. And because our culture is possessive, we think of it as something an individual possesses. But righteousness that an individual possesses is *self-righteousness*, . . . [which] the gospel says we cannot have (Romans 3).
>
> [In Matthew 5:6,] Jesus is alluding to Isaiah 61, which rejoices three times that God is bringing righteousness or justice. . . . The Hebrew *tsedaqah* . . . means *delivering justice* (a justice that rescues and releases the oppressed) and *community-restoring justice* (a justice that restores the powerless and the outcasts to their rightful place in covenant community). . . . That is why the hungry and the thirsty hunger and thirst for righteousness; they yearn bodily for the kind of justice that delivers them

from their hunger and thirst and restores them to community where they can eat and drink. It may be that only those . . . who have experienced injustice, hunger, and exclusion from community can fully experience the significance of what the Bible means by *justice*. But those are the kind of people who especially flocked to Jesus.[2]

This is why Jesus said we must *repent* if we want to enter into what the Kingdom of Heaven offers us. To confess "Jesus is Lord" is not a password to get into heaven. It is a declaration that we are submitting ourselves to the sovereign authority of Jesus in our lives and in the world. That's a game changer.

The gospel of the Kingdom of Heaven revolutionizes the way we live on earth and changes what we pursue. At the very core of the Good News of God's reign is that it creates a *Good News community* that seeks justice for all, not just righteousness for individuals.

The gospel is not individualistic. It is *communal*. Discipleship under the gospel of the Kingdom of Heaven demands that we live for the sake of others. This is why limiting our understanding of the gospel as primarily having to do with *individual conversion* is erroneous and degrades the glorious, life-changing effect of the gospel in the world.

Justice for the Neighborhood

Kurt Rietema is a revangelical. He is compelled by the Good News of God's reign to see the powerless ones in his community experience the "level ground" promised in Isaiah 40:4: "Fill in the valleys, and level the mountains and hills. Straighten the curves, and smooth out the rough places."[3]

Systems of injustice create valleys of despair and insurmountable mountains for some people (though they may look like mere molehills to those on top of the heap). Some systems are just plain crooked.

Soon after moving into an Argentine neighborhood in Kansas City, Kansas, Kurt and his wife, Emily, were touched by the kindness of their Hispanic neighbors, who shared food, watered their garden, and helped to landscape other neighbors' yards out of the kindness of their hearts. Kurt says, "All the grand illusions of my own generosity were shattered by living among Mexican immigrants who send half of their paychecks back home to their families in Mexico. And they're making way less than I am."

When Kurt learned of a "valley" that one of these Hispanic families was living in, his understanding of gospel righteousness and justice kicked into high gear. It meant he could not stand idly by. For several years, this immigrant family had been renting a home, but they had reached a point where the monthly cost was too great, and they were making plans to move. When Kurt discovered how much they were paying each month, he was appalled. They were being taken advantage of by an out-of-state corporation that owned huge numbers of houses like theirs across the country. Companies like these crisscross the nation, buying up troubled mortgages and turning them into cash cows that profit from the plight of lower-income and migrant families.

Kurt asked his neighbors if they had ever tried to buy their house. They said they had inquired a few years earlier, but the asking price was too steep. They told him the price they had been quoted, which Kurt felt was way too high. He volunteered to speak with the property manager on the family's behalf. Here is Kurt's account of what happened next:

I talked to the property manager and told her I hated to see my neighbors have to move away and asked if she thought the owners might be willing to sell the house. She said, "Well, the house is owned by a big conglomerate down in Texas, and it is really just a line item on their spreadsheet." She asked me what I thought the house was worth. I threw out a figure that was slightly more than one-third the price that had been quoted to my neighbors. Just a few days later, the property manager called me and said, "The seller accepted your offer."[4]

Kurt's first thought was, *Uh . . . I didn't make an offer.* But the faith-filled words that came out of his mouth were, "Okay, let's do it."

The logical place to turn for a home loan was a local mortgage company or bank. After inquiring about interest rates and associated fees for a mortgage loan, Kurt had a better idea:

I thought, *You know, I've got a lot of friends in some
area churches that are from the suburbs and would love
to get involved and help out in some way in the urban
corridor. I might be able to get a better rate for my
neighbors and create a good investment opportunity for
my friends.*

Kurt sent an e-mail to a few friends, and in no time several of them chipped in to invest and make the home loan.
Everybody won. His neighbors' monthly payment was cut
in half and they were on the road to becoming homeown-
ers. And the suburban partners were happy because they
were helping people out and getting a fair return on their
investment.

But the story doesn't end there. The house next door to
the one Kurt's friends had helped purchase was a drug house.
Kurt orchestrated the purchase of that house as well, and
some members of his neighbor's family bought it. Since then,
additional houses in the neighborhood have been purchased
under similar terms.

Kurt talks about the changes that have occurred in his
neighborhood:

In a place where people were once disconnected and
no one really knew or trusted one another, we began
to have this great community and we all began to
see *shalom* [peace] and stability coming into this
neighborhood that had seen so much blight and

turnover. It created a quality of depending on and trusting one another.

At the outset, the entire situation was twisted up in an issue of injustice and powerlessness. Kurt's neighbors were in a *valley*, and they had neither the means nor the connections to dig their way out. The system worked against this immigrant family. And even when a fair purchase price was within range, the cost of a bank loan was going to be higher for them because they were considered a greater risk. This was a situation that cried out for gospel justice, the righteousness of God.

When we choose to step into the Kingdom of Heaven, God brings heaven to earth, and it becomes a source of blessing for others and for ourselves. Kurt hungered and thirsted for righteousness (community-restoring justice) and both his family and the neighbors were filled.

The Evil Eye

It has been said that every point of view is a view from a point. This has to do with our perception of things. If you've ever been to the optometrist and looked through that contraption they use to sort out prescriptions for eyeglasses or contact lenses, you're familiar with the question, "Which is better, *one* or *two*?" The optometrist tries a variety of lens combinations and keeps asking the question—*one* or *two*?—until the proper prescription is determined and the patient can see correctly. Each of the Beatitudes is like one of those progressions—working and working until proper vision is achieved.

Jesus had a lot to say about vision. He had a lot to say about eyes. At the heart of the Sermon on the Mount, he talks about the issue of what we *treasure*. When our eyes and hearts are fixed on the Kingdom of Heaven, we hunger and thirst for the right things. We seek to store up treasure "where neither moth nor rust destroys and where thieves do not break in and steal" (Matthew 6:20).

Jesus also talks about our propensity to be anxious about clothing and food. He tells us to stop worrying about acquiring stuff. We have a loving father in heaven who will faithfully supply all of this for us. Jesus says, "Seek first the kingdom of God and his righteousness [justice], and all these [other] things will be added to you" (Matthew 6:33).

As my grandma would say, "Right flat dab in the middle" of his speech about treasuring the right things and the impossibility of serving God and money at the same time, Jesus throws in a statement about eyes and light:

> Your eye is a lamp that provides light for your body.
> When your eye is good, your whole body is filled
> with light. But when your eye is bad, your whole
> body is filled with darkness. And if the light you
> think you have is actually darkness, how deep that
> darkness is!
>
> MATTHEW 6:22-23, NLT

Recently, when I was watching a PBS documentary about space exploration and astronomy, the subject turned to some of the great observatories and giant telescopes throughout the world. One of the scientists interviewed said that most people believe large telescopes are needed for greater magnification of the stars and planets. But that's not the case. The large telescopes are actually needed because they capture as much light as possible. The more light that can be captured, the clearer the image will be.

Jesus says we must be certain that we're seeing correctly and getting plenty of light into ourselves. It is difficult to sift our paradigms and ideologies from the truth of the gospel. Much of what we've come to believe (our cultural norms) seems to us to be unquestionably true, especially when our parents and elders in the faith have walked in a certain understanding and passed it down to us.

Fuller Seminary president Mark Labberton says,

ONE OF THE MOST PROBLEMATICAL PARTS OF ORDINARY discipleship is that it is more likely to be an expression of our sociology than our Christology. That is, we are more prone to see people and events through the lens of our background, class, ethnicity, or more, rather than through the lens of Jesus' compassion, justice, and mercy. This is not a surprise, of course. It is just that too often we don't realize how much deeper the transformative work of the gospel must be since our own sociological lenses leave us with vision that is often so distorted and self-serving, even blind.[5]

Jesus warns us of the mistake of thinking that what we have is light (correct understanding), when all along it is actually darkness. Only then does he return to warning us about not seeking earthly treasure.

That's Not Fair

When Christians view life from a worldly point of view, the result is a gospel blindness that fails to see beyond cultural norms to envision much greater possibilities. The attitudes of some evangelicals when they post their opinions on social media or speak about the issues of immigration and the poor are both appalling and shameful. Such dark heartedness runs contrary to the righteous justice that Jesus speaks of in the Beatitudes.

In the days immediately following the 2012 presidential election, conservative media personality Bill O'Reilly gave his explanation for Barack Obama's reelection. "The demographics are changing," he said. "It's not a traditional America anymore. [And these untraditional Americans] want stuff. They want things. And who is going to give them things? President Obama. He knows it, and he ran on it."[6]

Evangelicals across America said a hearty "amen" to O'Reilly's remarks. The dividing line in the presidential election was widely defined by conservatives (including many evangelicals) as an issue of "makers vs. takers." Snarky and demeaning jokes were often heard, even among those who claim to follow Jesus, the greatest advocate the poor have ever had. Every time I heard or read caustic remarks about the poor from Christians, the words of Solomon rang in my head: "Those who mock the poor insult their Maker."[7]

In Matthew 20:1-16, Jesus tells the parable of an estate owner who went out early one morning to hire workers for his vineyard. This scene can be easily imagined today. Most cities have known locations where day laborers gather, hoping to be hired by construction and landscape bosses. In Jesus' story, the laborers agree with the vineyard owner to work for a standard day's wage and are put to work.

> At nine o'clock in the morning he was passing through the marketplace and saw some people standing around doing nothing. So he hired them, telling them he would pay them whatever was right at the end of the day. So they went to work in the vineyard. At noon and again at three o'clock he did the same thing.
>
> At five o'clock that afternoon he was in town again and saw some more people standing around. He asked them, "Why haven't you been working today?"
>
> They replied, "Because no one hired us."
>
> The landowner told them, "Then go out and join the others in my vineyard."
>
> MATTHEW 20:3-7, NLT

Notice that the reason these people weren't working was because they hadn't been offered a job. It wasn't because they were lazy. As soon as they were presented an opportunity, they jumped at it.

This is where the story takes a turn. Tensions are about to rise. At the end of the day, *all* of the laborers, regardless of when they'd been hired, received a full day's wage. Those who had started the workday early in the morning were beside themselves. They couldn't believe that others had received the same wage for working just part of the day—and some had been hired not long before quitting time. But the laborers who had worked all day received exactly what they had agreed to. And it was a fair wage—the going rate. The vineyard owner rebuked these workers for their "sour grapes" viewpoint and attitude. He said, "Is your eye evil because I am good?" (Matthew 20:15, NKJV). So we see that Jesus has a term to describe the hardhearted inclination to resent generosity. He calls it an "evil eye."

Looking back at what Jesus says in Matthew 6:22-23, if we find ourselves resentful, hard-hearted, and critical toward those of lesser means, perhaps we should pause to consider whether the light we think we have is actually darkness.

The "light" metaphor is all about *perception* and *understanding*. Jesus tells us that we had better make sure our understanding (light) on matters is correct. If our understanding, or viewpoint, is incorrect, then we are walking in darkness rather than in the light. Jesus calls it an evil eye, which means we have a wicked viewpoint.

An example of how darkness is mistaken for light can be seen in the misuse of a familiar text from 2 Thessalonians. Writing about a 2013 gathering of the House Agriculture

Committee to discuss whether or not to cut more than $4 billion from the Supplemental Nutrition Assistance Program (SNAP, formerly known as food stamps), blogger Jack Jenkins writes,

> As House members discussed slashing the budget for the Farm Bill, which funds SNAP, Rep. Stephen Fincher (R-TN) took issue with some Democrats who cited Jesus Christ's call to care for "the least of these" when describing the government's need to assist the hungry. Instead, Fincher explained his support for the proposed cuts by quoting a very different Bible verse—2 Thessalonians 3:10: "For even when we were with you, we gave you this command: Anyone unwilling to work should not eat."
>
> But while 2 Thessalonians is a convenient tool for those who want to justify ignoring the poor, Fincher's lukewarm biblical argument doesn't hold up under scrutiny. . . . The author of 2 Thessalonians was actually referring to ancient Christians who had stopped working in anticipation of Jesus' Second Coming. The verse is concerned with correcting a theological misunderstanding (i.e., don't just wait around for Jesus, live an active faith), not passing judgment on the poor.[8]

Jesus instructs us to seek our treasure in heaven (Matthew 6:20), which is the realm of God's reign and rule. In that context, he tells us to make seeking God's Kingdom and his righteousness—his restorative justice—our first priority. But in practice, the *seeking* he calls for often gets sidetracked by our seeking of our own best interests.

In the parable of the sower (Matthew 13:3-23), Jesus says the seed sown among thorns is a metaphor for someone "who hears the word, but the cares of the world and the deceitfulness of riches choke the word, and it proves unfruitful" in that person's life.[9] This happens when our concern for our own stuff keeps us from letting the words of Jesus take root in our hearts. Sure, we allow certain things that Jesus says to grow and live in our lives, but there's a lot that we just don't seem to take seriously. When the Kingdom of God stuff is suffocated by our self-interest, the possibility for living in a more open-handed way gets smothered as well.

Self-Made Men and Women?

Many evangelicals (especially white evangelicals) grew up like I did. We weren't rich by American standards, though by the standards of 98 percent of the world we were wealthy. The opportunity to get an education, and even a higher education, was within our means—if we really wanted it.

Many middle-class evangelicals are of the mind that most *everybody* in America stands at the same point they do. Therefore, the reason people are poor must be because they are lazy and don't want to work, or at least they don't want to work hard enough to make things better for themselves.

In some cases this might be true. There will always be

a few people who are unmotivated and will mooch off the goodwill of others. But these are far from the majority of the poor among us. Stereotyping the poor is strictly forbidden in Scripture.

When new interns arrive for our church planters' training in Kansas City, one of the first things we do is drive them down Troost Avenue, the line of demarcation in the city. Troost Avenue separates the haves from the have-nots, the hopeful from the hopeless. The demographic differences from one side of the street to the other are a portrait of complete opposites—not only in regard to race, but also education, income, and household stability.

I set the U2 song "Where the Streets Have No Name" on a loop on my car stereo and tell the church planters to just look and listen. I'm not going to say a word, and I don't want them to say anything either. As we proceed down Troost, I turn east for a block or two and pass by a stark and blighted elementary school. Then I turn around, crossing over Troost again, and drive a couple of blocks to the west, passing another elementary school. But this school is nothing like the first one. It is bright, up to date, welcoming, and lively. It might as well be in a different world.

As Bono continues to sing and the contrasts begin to sink in, I turn the car around and drive east, crossing Troost Avenue again. Within a couple of blocks, we pass by a public park where paint peels from dilapidated playground equipment on a sun-scorched, grassless sandlot. I immediately turn west again, crossing Troost and driving by another public park. This one is carpeted in plush green grass surrounding a beautifully manicured lake, with one of Kansas City's famed fountains spewing a watery stream from the center. Bright and colorful state-of-the-art playground equipment stands at the ready for eager children to squeal in delighted fun and joy.

It usually takes only about ten minutes to do this tour. Almost every time, at the end of the drive, when I look at the young men in my car, I see tears streaming down their cheeks. Without a word being spoken, these guys understand that the playing field is not level.

It would be absurd and hard-hearted for anyone to suggest that the children who grow up on the east side of Troost Avenue (or in countless similar neighborhoods across the country) have the same opportunities as those on the west side. The atmosphere of inequality alone breeds despair and hopelessness.

I know that many people have grown up in poverty and have overcome the obstacles. But poverty poses significant challenges to a child's development. For example, proper nutrition is essential for good health. But healthy foods are unaffordable for many poor people. Children born into poor families often arrive at lower birth weights, have no health coverage, and start school not ready to learn. They quickly fall behind and become prime dropout candidates.

Schools in lower-income neighborhoods are more likely to employ teachers with less experience, fewer advanced degrees, and limited access to ongoing training. Clearly, the children they teach are not getting a fair chance to learn the skills and knowledge they will need in order to compete and thrive in our society.

When we suggest that the economically poor are just unwilling to "pull themselves up by their bootstraps," we expose our own callous hearts. We have failed to look closely enough to realize that these people don't even have boots, much less straps to grab on to.

We have missed the blessedness of being "poor in spirit" by identifying with the poor. To be poor in spirit is to realize our utter dependency on God from start to finish. It is to be completely humbled in gratitude, realizing that everything, everything, *everything* we have was given to us by God. Does the child born on one side of town *deserve* to be born there and not on the other side of the tracks? Of course not. Children born on the *wrong* side of town did not place themselves in that mess, any more than the children born into stable, upper-middle-class, white evangelical families chose the circumstances of *their* birth. We need to be awakened by the words of Tim Keller, who writes, "When Christians who understand the gospel see a poor person, they realize they are looking into a mirror. Their hearts must go out to him or her without an ounce of superiority or indifference."[10]

Valleys of despair become the dwelling places of those who suffer at the expense of others who are living on mountains of excess. During election seasons, the loudest message going out to the world from the conservative side is usually not, "Who will help us look out for the needs of 'the least of these' among us?" but rather, "Who will make sure we hold on to what we have worked hard for and rightfully deserve?"

The Hebrew and Greek words for *justice* are used more than one thousand times in the Bible. Compare that with the words for *sexual sin*, which are used fewer than one hundred times. Now when you consider the anxiety and obsession with sexual issues of the typical contemporary evangelical, you've pretty much set the stage for what Jesus said to the Pharisees of his day:

> What sorrow awaits you teachers of religious law
> and you Pharisees. Hypocrites! For you are careful to
> tithe even the tiniest income from your herb gardens,
> but you ignore the more important aspects of the
> law—justice, mercy, and faith. You should tithe, yes,
> but do not neglect the more important things. Blind
> guides! You strain your water so you won't accidentally
> swallow a gnat, but you swallow a camel!
>
> MATTHEW 23:23-24, NLT

At the beginning of this chapter, we looked at how most English versions of the Bible translate the word for *justice* as "righteousness." But by now it should be easy to see that the majority of evangelicals have largely overlooked or ignored the Bible's tenacity on the topic of *justice*, and the central role it plays in Jesus' Kingdom agenda.

Many evangelical churches have spent enormous amounts of time, energy, and money demanding "righteousness" under the rubric of prayer in public schools, returning the Ten Commandments to the walls of our courthouses, or (the latest) preserving "the sanctity of marriage," while the outcry on behalf of the oppressed and a tangible pursuit of justice for the poor has languished.

I don't want to trivialize these heartfelt issues. For example, I am all for prayer in public schools. But the surefire way to put prayer back in the public schools is to actually pray for our schools by lifting up teachers, students, and school administrators, and by training our children to be praying people themselves. No one can keep prayer out of schools. We need to keep our focus on what is truly important. In the first place, Jesus told us not to make a show of public prayer, but to approach our heavenly Father in private.

> When you come before God, don't turn that into a theatrical production either. All these people making a regular show out of their prayers, hoping for stardom! Do you think God sits in a box seat?
>
> Here's what I want you to do: Find a quiet, secluded place so you won't be tempted to role-play before God. Just be there as simply and honestly as you can manage. The focus will shift from you to God, and you will begin to sense his grace.
>
> MATTHEW 6:5-6, MSG

Likewise, it seems to me that the best way to preserve "the sanctity of marriage" is for Christians to have great marriages and do more to keep their covenants together. By displaying the blessings of obediently following Jesus, we bear witness to his ways and means. When, year by year, statistics reveal the divorce rate among professing Christians to be neck and neck with those who make no claims of following Christ, it seems that the "sanctity" of marriage has already been called into question.

This is where the greatness of genuine Christianity shines. There is no law that can stop us from living out the gospel of the Kingdom of Heaven.

Laws still matter, of course. But which laws should we focus on changing?

On our way to Target or P. F. Chang's or to grab our daily five-dollar latte, we drive past predatory storefront title loan companies that suffocate the vulnerable poor with legalized interest rates as high as 200 to 300 percent.[11] Quite often, we pass by these loan sharks on our way to consume more stuff from a corporation that hides its workers' tears behind smiley-face advertisements and the promise of lower prices. Where is the evangelical angst and rage over such abuse?

We should turn in our Bibles to what might be the most terrifying of Jesus' teachings—the portrait he paints of the final judgment (Matthew 25:31-46). In that scene, the sheep are separated from the goats—but not based on their track record of prophesying, exorcising demons, or performing miracles. Not based on their record of memorizing Scripture or keeping the biblical laws. Not based on their church attendance, style of worship, or views on spiritual gifts. Rather,

Jesus says the true sheep will be known by how they cared for "the least of these," for those who are in need and on the margins of society.

Are the Poor Lazy?

Jesus expects his Good News people to stand in one accord with those who are powerless, poor, and concealed in the weeds at the edges of society's byways. Too often, the opposite is true. The attitudes of evangelicals are frequently tainted with predetermined judgments and stereotypes. One of the more common misnomers about the poor is that they are mostly lazy and unmotivated to work. But according to the US Department of Labor, 10.4 million people in our nation live in poverty while participating in the labor force.[12] These are the ones categorized as the "working poor."

> In 2010, 7 percent of those aged 16 and older who
> worked some or all of the year were in poverty.
> And the Department of Agriculture reported that
> 30 percent of households receiving food assistance
> had earnings in 2010; 41 percent of food aid
> beneficiaries lived in a household with earnings from
> a job. Nearly a quarter—21.8 percent—of non-
> elderly adult food stamp recipients were employed.[13]

Consider those who work for Walmart. Not only is Walmart America's largest private employer, but it also has the most workers on public assistance. In 2007, as the great recession clamped down, Walmart made a change from regular work shifts to flexible shifts. This bumped many full-time workers to part-time status. On top of losing work hours, they were no longer eligible for health insurance and other benefits. As a consequence, hundreds of thousands of Walmart employees were pushed into line for Medicaid and other government benefits.[14]

Economists have coined the term "Walmart Syndrome" to describe similar practices by other big-name corporations, such as McDonald's. According to a July 2012 report from the National Employment Law Project, 26 percent of the private sector jobs in the United States pay less than $10 per hour.[15]

Who ultimately pays the price? Besides the low-wage workers themselves, who can't afford to live on what they make, it's US taxpayers—the same people who think they're getting such great daily deals by shopping at those stores—who make up the gap through government welfare payments to the tune of close to $90 billion per year.[16] The winners are the corporate executives, whose pay has increased 127 times faster than the pay of the average worker over the past thirty years.[17]

Most likely, over the past week, you and I were served by hardworking people who are on the edge of poverty. The retail store clerk, the fast-food worker, the middle-aged pizza delivery man are all part of almost 50 million Americans who live in families where someone is working but still falling short of the poverty line of $23,021 for a family of four. Most of these people live from paycheck to paycheck. Many of them work more than one job while raising children. One car breakdown or medical emergency can send them into a financial tailspin.

During the time my wife worked as a clerk at Target, she worked with a Hispanic man in his fifties who was laboring to support his family. Unable to get one full-time job, his warehouse job at Target was but one of three part-time jobs he reported to daily.

When the topic of raising taxes on the upper middle class comes up for discussion, one of the objections raised (often from conservative white evangelicals) is that the poor don't pay taxes. But that's not true. Though they may not earn enough to pay federal income tax, the working poor pay federal payroll taxes and sales taxes at the same rate as everyone else.

> Under tax programs that both Republicans and Democrats supported as a way to get poor people off welfare, workers with low incomes qualify for the Earned Income Tax Credit and often the Child Tax Credit. Perversely, however, these special tax breaks serve as disincentives for the working poor to make more money. A single mother earning $18,000 a year loses tax credits and benefits as she climbs the income scale, so for each additional dollar she makes, she effectively keeps only 12 cents. She has little incentive to increase her hours and her income unless she can make a major jump in salary.[18]

Even those of us traditionally categorized as middle class feel the crushing pressure of a crooked and broken system. Look no further than the recent mortgage crisis that left millions of Americans in foreclosure. These folks lost their homes while the corporate heads, with their government bailouts and golden parachutes, barely skipped a beat.

As revangelicals, how should our hearts be inclined toward the poor? As purveyors of the good news of Christ's reign, should our attitudes be different from those of non-Christ followers—people who make no claim to being citizens of the Kingdom of God? If we claim to be followers of Jesus, we will seek to bring his presence and attitude to bear in every situation of life.

The scribes, Pharisees, and chief priests were obsessed with appearing to be morally pure and righteous. Jesus was obsessed with purity of heart, compassion toward the broken, and release of cultural captives. When discussions surface about fair distribution of resources, I am both saddened and amazed when evangelicals scream, "Socialism! Marxism!" It causes me to look back eighty years to the words of E. Stanley Jones, words that could have been penned this morning:

> I am not a Communist, nor do I call myself a
> Socialist, but I am a Christian seeking for a solution
> to this problem. I am sure—desperately sure—
> that Christianity must give a lead at this place or
> abdicate. It is not enough to tell me that Christianity
> can and does change the lives of individual men.

I know it, and am grateful beyond words for that fact. But it is not enough. Shall we rescue individual slaves and leave intact the slave system? . . . Shall we pick up the wounded in war and leave intact the war system? Shall we pick up the derelicts of a competitive system and give them doles and leave the system to go on producing its poverty, its hates, and its exploiting imperialisms?[19]

If we want to become Good News to the world, we must be re-evangelized by the gospel of Jesus. Our hearts and attitudes toward the poor must seek *first* the reign of God and *his* idea of righteousness—justice for all (Matthew 6:33).

Jesus didn't tell us to "agree with his concepts." He called us to *engage* them. He told us to look for manifestations of the Kingdom of Heaven and justice. This is not a passive posture. It is a position of *pursuit*; it means actually taking steps to see the justice of the Kingdom happen.

The first hurdle we must clear centers on the evangelical heart. If we are going to be biblically *just* people (that is, *righteous*), we must be willing to disadvantage ourselves in order to raise the valley floor for the entire community. The opposite is true for unjust people—evangelical or otherwise. They are more than happy to see others disadvantaged as long as they themselves can live on the mountaintop.

Good News Kingdom of Heaven people see their dollars as not belonging to themselves. They reject the nonbiblical attitude that says, "I earned it and it's mine. I tithe and pay my taxes. I do my part and don't want anyone touching what is mine." Some Christians might be astonished to discover that such an attitude runs contrary to the Kingdom economy.

Geoff and Sherry Maddock are revangelicals who live in the core of a broken neighborhood. They are highly educated people, both holding seminary degrees, who took the concept of *gleanings* quite literally when they established a garden around their urban home in Lexington, Kentucky. The house is on a corner lot, and many people walk past each day. There's also a city bus stop just a few feet away. The Maddocks strategically positioned their berry bushes for the enjoyment of anyone who happens to be nearby. They've even placed a little sign inviting people to partake at will. Geoff and Sherry harvest the yard side of the bushes and leave the street side for the gleaners.

Their home has become a neighborhood beacon as they have become essential cogs in the "re-neighboring" of the community in which they live. Geoff and Sherry helped to start a faith community called Communality. They live and work as missionaries, tethered to their intentional community with an outward orientation to serve the world around them. Helped by their education in mission and evangelism from Asbury Seminary, they have built relationships across racial, cultural, and socioeconomic boundaries. Their day-to-day work finds them assisting refugees in resettlement, advocating for the poor, promoting and enacting racial reconciliation, and living sustainably through community gardens and other creation care initiatives.

The principle of providing *gleanings* was established by God. He told his people to leave the unharvested edges of their crop fields available for the poor and for migrants, and not to go back over the trees and crops to make sure every last bit of fruit had been gathered. He said to leave it for the poor.

> When you are harvesting your crops and forget to bring in a bundle of grain from your field, don't go back to get it. Leave it for the foreigners, orphans, and widows. Then the LORD your God will bless you in all you do. When you beat the olives from your olive trees, don't go over the boughs twice. Leave the remaining olives for the foreigners, orphans, and widows. When you gather the grapes in your vineyard, don't glean the vines after they are picked. Leave the remaining grapes for the foreigners, orphans, and widows.
>
> DEUTERONOMY 24:19-21, NLT

In the eyes of the Lord, a portion of every Israelite's hard-earned "paycheck" belonged to the poor and dispossessed. This was all part of God's plan for his people to be a blessing to the world around them. Israel was a foreshadowing of the church—the people of God called to be a blessing in the midst of a host culture.

The Lord has called his followers to join him in demonstrating *his* brand of righteousness. If you're like me, you may have thought righteousness was just an individual issue. But it is far grander than that. Seeing as Jesus sees—and wants *us* to see—clears our eyes. When our eyes are clear, Jesus says, our entire bodies will be engulfed with light. That is, when we see the world clearly, as Jesus does, our lives will naturally overflow with works of righteousness, bringing heavenly justice, healing, and restoration into our fallen world.

To not only *see* the poor, oppressed, and downtrodden, but to stand in solidarity with them, is to enter into the blessedness of being "poor in spirit." By pursuing a living wage for everyone, as one example, revangelicals can be proactive in seeking outcomes that straighten the crooked ways and fill in the gaps on the unlevel playing fields. Biblical justice for the poor and for immigrants is not communism or socialism. Biblical justice is the righteousness of Jesus. We might just call it Jesusism.

QUESTIONS FOR REFLECTION

1. Before reading this chapter, what was your concept or definition of *righteousness*? How about your definition of *justice*? How have your views been challenged or changed by this chapter?

2. How does the biblical idea of justice place demands on you as an evangelical—that is, as a *Good News* Christian?

3. As it pertains to your posture toward justice for the poor, where do you see yourself on the following continuum? How has your perspective been influenced by this chapter?

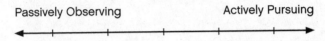

Passively Observing   Actively Pursuing

4. How have you perceived the poor through the lens of your own background, personal economic concerns, and social status? How does this differ from the "Jesusian" lens of compassion, justice, and mercy?

5. When you consider economic policies, are you most concerned with how they affect you and your stuff or how they may affect the poor?

6. What issues of injustice are you aware of in your community? How might you participate in bringing God's righteousness to bear on these situations?

8

REUNITE

When he drew near and saw the city, he wept over it, saying,
"Would that you, even you, had known on this day the things
that make for peace! But now they are hidden from your eyes."

LUKE 19:41-42

MY FIRST FORAY into the cause of peacemaking was at a
keg party in high school. A couple of my friends, Zac and
Brett, were gassed on liquid courage and began fighting.
Really fighting. They were scratching, clawing, pulling hair,
and I remember some biting going on as well. The rest of
my buddies were standing by watching, as if it were a pay-
per-view event. I was seriously worried that one of the guys
was going to get badly injured, and I said to a couple of
my friends, "Hey, we've gotta break this up. They're going
to kill each other." Kevin and Johnny both gave nods of
agreement, so I stepped in between the two combatants,

expecting the other guys to pull Zac and Brett away from each other. But as I plunged into the fray, Kevin and Johnny just stood there.

It took me about thirty seconds to extricate myself from between the two sets of fists that were now pummeling my head from both sides. After shaking out the cobwebs from my ringing ears, I shouted at Kevin and Johnny above the rowdy crowd and Lynyrd Skynyrd blaring from a nearby stereo, "Come on, help me out here!"

They both nodded in agreement . . . again.

Deciding to take a different tack this time, I grabbed Zac from behind, pulling both his arms down in a bear hug. I expected one of my buddies to do the same to Brett, but as before, I was left alone in the intervention. This time, I wasn't the one to pay the price. With his arms pinned behind him, Zac became a defenseless punching bag.

After it was all over, a thoroughly drunk and dazed Zac said to Kevin and Johnny, "I was just about to take him, but some #$%! grabbed my arms. Who was that? I'm gonna kick his—"

Peacemaking can be dangerous business. Genuine peacemaking goes beyond merely *advocating* for peace. It means *taking action*. I have discovered time and again that taking a peacemaking stance does not give me immunity from attack. Peacemaking is a subject that, ironically, can stir people up to verbal violence. What I find disconcerting is how quickly it can agitate some Christians to serious fits of anger.

I once got into a Facebook discussion with a childhood

friend who became so incensed with my views of peace that he wrote, "What Jesus are you following!?" Imagine that. I was making an argument for *less* war and less *celebration* of war, and my evangelical friend challenged my concept of Jesus. I was stunned.

I'm not about to attempt a full-blown treatise on the subject of peacemaking here. That would be foolhardy. For example, I'm not going to debate gun control or "just war" theory, or whether or not Christians should join the military. Complete volumes have been written on those subjects. What I want to focus on in this chapter is the state of the evangelical heart and our attitude toward the issue of peace. How should a follower of Jesus feel about war and violence?

The Heart of the Matter

Jesus was just as concerned with *why* his followers would do something as he was about *what* they did. He knew that the problems of the world could never be changed with moral rules and regulations that started with outside behavior. Certain and lasting change would have to begin with the human heart. Just after listing the Beatitudes during his Sermon on the Mount, Jesus says,

> You have heard that our ancestors were told, "You must not murder. If you commit murder, you are subject to judgment." But I say, if you are even angry with someone, you are subject to judgment! If you

> call someone an idiot, you are in danger of being
> brought before the court. And if you curse someone,
> you are in danger of the fires of hell.
>
> MATTHEW 5:21-22, NLT

Jesus raised the bar on what he expected from his followers. He didn't just want moral actions and compliance with external laws. He wanted good-hearted people. The word Jesus used for "idiot" is the Aramaic word *raca*—which sounds a lot like clearing one's throat before spitting. That also captures the meaning of the word, which is to view someone with deep contempt. To call someone *raca* was tantamount to spitting in the person's face.

Jesus says that murder begins with devaluing another person. That is, to call someone an *idiot* comes from the same spirit that causes people to commit murder. Jesus makes no distinction about the recipient of such hatred— it might be a politician, a foreigner, a person from another race, or someone who opposes our moral or theological beliefs—but he gives an incredibly stern warning about defiling someone's personhood: "You are in danger of the fires of hell."

When Christians lower themselves to name-calling, joke-making, and snarky remarks about those they oppose, not only are they breaking the fundamental tenets of the faith, but they are also stepping outside the realm of God's reign into a lower order. It is not wisdom from the Kingdom of Heaven.

The wisdom from above is first of all pure. It is also peace loving, gentle at all times, and willing to yield to others. It is full of mercy and good deeds. It shows no favoritism and is always sincere. And those who are peacemakers will plant seeds of peace and reap a harvest of righteousness.

JAMES 3:17-18, NLT

The apostle James says that heavenly wisdom is manifested in people who are *peace loving*. A calming gentleness exudes from heavenly wise people. They plant seeds of peace wherever they go. Wisdom from the Kingdom of Heaven shows no favoritism—including the political kind.

When we love someone or something, we do all we can for them. One of the primary marks of a true evangelical—a *Good News* person—should be an all-out love of peace. My concern is that many Christians today do not *love* peace. They sort of like it. They're all for it whenever it happens. But they don't *love* it to the extent that they try to *make* it happen. Evangelicals have an extremely poor track record in the arena of *making* peace. In a survey taken just prior to the beginning of the Iraq war, 69 percent of conservative Christians supported military action in Baghdad. This Christian advocacy for war was a full 10 percent higher than in the general US population.[1]

For Christians to get hyped up and invigorated about vigilante justice on stateside streets or military operations on foreign battlefields is incompatible with the Jesus of the New

Testament. Those who lay claim to the name of the Prince of Peace should not be rejoicing at reports of foreign war casualties or the execution of a convict. Those are times for mourning with those who mourn, including the families of the "bad guys" or "the enemy."

How can we who believe there is hell after death for the godless say, "He got what he deserved," when a life is ended? Attitudes such as these are as different as oil and water in light of the character and persona of Jesus.

The Making of Peace

Let's take a look at just a few verses from the New Testament that speak to our response to evil:

Never pay back evil with more evil. Do things in such a way that everyone can see you are honorable. Do all that you can to live in peace with everyone.
Dear friends, never take revenge. Leave that to the righteous anger of God. For the Scriptures say,

"I will take revenge;
    I will pay them back,"
    says the LORD.

Instead,

"If your enemies are hungry, feed them.
    If they are thirsty, give them something to drink.

In doing this, you will heap
    burning coals of shame on their heads."

Don't let evil conquer you, but conquer evil by doing
good.
ROMANS 12:17-21, NLT

See that no one repays anyone evil for evil, but always
seek to do good to one another and to everyone.
1 THESSALONIANS 5:15

For God called you to do good, even if it means
suffering, just as Christ suffered for you. He is your
example, and you must follow in his steps.

He never sinned,
    nor ever deceived anyone.
He did not retaliate when he was insulted,
    nor threaten revenge when he suffered.
He left his case in the hands of God,
    who always judges fairly.

1 PETER 2:21-23, NLT

A clear and consistent theme comes through in these verses:
Break the cycle of retaliation and revenge by responding with
goodness.

Jesus ushered in a *transformation* from the earthly ways
of living to the heavenly ways of the Kingdom of God. His

means was *love*. Not just in word, but also in deed. People often mistake *pacifism* for *passivism*. Passivism means to not react. Passivists are inactive, idle, inert, supine. Pacifism is not like that at all. In fact, it means "*strongly* and *actively* opposed to conflict."[2] Pacifists are advocates of *peaceful resolution*. As such, every Christian should be a pacifist. The word *pacifist* is synonymous with *peacemaker*.

Love does not merely step aside. It doesn't stop at "Don't return evil for evil." Rather, it moves forward, proactively, returning *good* for evil. The Silver Rule says, "Don't do to others what you don't want them to do to you." But that's not the biblical standard of measure. The Golden Rule—the rule that Jesus lived by and taught—is so much higher: "Do unto others as you would have them do unto you."[3]

The essence of living in accordance with the Kingdom of Heaven is that we lay down (surrender) our own forms of power, in favor of actively *waging peace*. The irony is that the Kingdom approach does not bring bondage to our lives; it actually creates the widest spaces of freedom we can imagine. For one thing, we're set free from foraging in the fields of human competition. Scholar Johann Metz writes:

> It is not a liberation from our powerlessness, but from our own form of predominance. It frees us, not from the state of being dominated but from that of dominating; not from our sufferings but from our apathy; not from our guilt but from our innocence, or rather from that delusion of

innocence which the life of domination has long
since spread out through our souls.[4]

Resisting Evil

For the first couple of decades of my own journey of
Christianity, whenever I read verses about the lion lying
down with the lamb, or swords being remade into plowshares and spears into pruning hooks, I viewed these ideas
sentimentally, as ethereal concepts. It never occurred to me to
actually *live* that way. But that is precisely how Jesus intends
for his followers to live. In Matthew 5:38-39, Jesus says to
the crowd, "You have heard that it was said, 'An eye for an eye
and a tooth for a tooth.' But I say to you, Do not resist the
one who is evil. But if anyone slaps you on the right cheek,
turn to him the other also."

Do not resist an evil person. Really? That doesn't jibe with
what we see Jesus doing in Scripture. He constantly resisted
evil people. Just look at his numerous confrontations with the
scribes and Pharisees. He even rebuked and resisted Peter on
more than one occasion. So, what are we not understanding in
Jesus' statement? The difference lies in *how* Jesus resisted evil.

Clarence Jordan, whose ministry laid the groundwork for
Habitat for Humanity, worked in the Deep South and was
on the front lines of the battle for civil rights. He points out
that the Greek word for *evil* can be interpreted as "by evil
means" or "the evil person."[5] The context in which the word
is used is what determines the meaning. So in the context of
how Jesus dealt with people and evil, it is obvious that he did

not resist evil by using evil means. New Testament scholar William Hendriksen adds to our understanding:

> The Old Testament repeatedly forbids personal vengeance: "You shall not take vengeance, nor bear any grudge against the children of your people; you shall love your neighbor as yourself; I am Jehovah" (Levi. 19:18). "Do not say, I will repay evil. Wait for Jehovah, and he will save you" (Prov. 20:22). "Do not say, as he has done to me so will I do to him; I will pay the man back according to what he has done" (Prov. 24:29).
>
> What then did Jesus mean when he said, "Do not resist the evil-doer" . . . etc.? When Christ's words (verses 39-42) are read in the light of what immediately *follows* in verses 43-48, and when the parallel in Luke 6:29, 30 is explained on the basis of what immediately *precedes* in verses 27, 28, it becomes clear that the key passage, identical in both Gospels, is "Love your enemies" (Matt. 5:44; Luke 6:27). In other words, Jesus is condemning the spirit of lovelessness, hatred, yearning for revenge. He is saying, "Do not resist the evil-doer with measures that arise from an unloving, unforgiving, unrelenting, vindictive disposition."[6]

Let's look at how this form of resistance applies to what is possibly the most troubling thing Jesus said in relation to our natural inclinations: "If anyone slaps you on the right cheek, turn to him the other also."[7]

Now, find that thinking cap and put it on again. You must picture this clearly in your mind.

In the days of Jesus, it was widely known that to slap someone on the right cheek with the back of one's hand was meant as an insult. It conveyed a clear message: "I am your superior." Think of those scenes in old movies where a military officer uses his gloves to slap an inferior. The *insult* was meant to bring more pain than the physical blow.

Also, in the Middle East during Jesus' time, as is still the custom today, the left hand was considered unclean because it was used for cleansing after using the toilet. One was never to eat with the left hand or to strike someone with the left hand.

So if I were standing face to face with you, the only way I could slap you on your *right* cheek would be to backhand you with my right hand. If you turned to offer your *left* cheek, the only way I could strike you would be to either use my left hand, which would degrade *me*, or to slug you with my right hand. But to strike someone with a straight-on punch would elevate that person as an equal and worthy opponent. Either way, I am in a pickle. So if you "turn the other cheek," I can't keep you below me in status. Jesus was not advocating passivity. He was advocating nonviolent confrontation.

Examples of nonviolent confrontation happened regularly during the 1960s civil rights struggle. As Glen Stassen points out, "The civil rights movement followed a strategy called 'direct action.' . . . A small group of blacks and whites would enter a segregated restaurant together and sit down to be served. Thus they would desegregate the restaurant directly until they were arrested. Then they turned the other cheek by serving time in jail rather than paying bail."[8]

The Sword of Jesus

One phrase that Jesus used a lot was, "He who has ears to hear, let him hear."[9] So much of what he said was in a Kingdom of Heaven dialect, which requires an understanding of Jesus' hidden meanings. So when he told his disciples to "beware of the leaven of the Pharisees and Sadducees," they thought he was telling them to be careful when eating bread from those religious leaders. But Jesus later explained that "leaven" was an analogy for the *teaching* of the Pharisees and Sadducees.[10]

In Matthew 10:34, Jesus says, "Do not think that I have come to bring peace to the earth. I have not come to bring peace, but a sword." In Luke's version of this same statement, he quotes Jesus as saying, "Do you think that I have come to give peace on earth? No, I tell you, but rather division."[11] So the *sword* of Jesus is not meant to be a literal sword. The sword represents the division brought about by the gospel of the Kingdom of Heaven. Likewise, the Cross is a place of division. It divides the ways of heaven from the ways of earth. It offends our sensibilities and causes a war in our hearts. It doesn't bring us peace at the beginning; it stirs division between our ways and God's ways. The Word and the Cross bring distinction between our fleshly and heavenly perspectives. See what the writer of Hebrews says:

The word of God is alive and powerful. It is sharper
than the sharpest two-edged sword, cutting between
soul and spirit, between joint and marrow. It exposes
our innermost thoughts and desires.

HEBREWS 4:12, NLT

The Cross stands for overcoming hatred and evil with goodness and love. It meets the weapons of force with the weapons of kindness, compassion, and generosity. In the words
of Jesus,

Love your enemies! Do good to them. Lend to them
without expecting to be repaid. Then your reward
from heaven will be very great, and you will truly
be acting as children of the Most High, for he is
kind to those who are unthankful and wicked. You
must be compassionate, just as your Father is
compassionate.

LUKE 6:35-36, NLT

The gospel of the Kingdom threatens all power that is
not of itself. It critiques cultures, institutions, ideologies, ethics, and individuals. Jesus said that the one who lives by the
sword will die by the sword. His means and ends are always
in complete agreement. Jesus brings peace by the use of
peace. But this wreaks havoc on our fleshly ways and means.
The very idea of peacemaking threatens our natural inclination to fight back.

Most of the major English translations render Matthew 5:9, Jesus' declaration about peacemaking in the Sermon on the Mount, in a way similar to the King James Version: "Blessed are the peacemakers: for they shall be called the children of God." The phrase "they shall be called the children of God" falls short of evoking the intended meaning because the word *children* gives the notion of little ones. But the Greek word here is *huios*, which means "direct offspring." Jesus is saying that when we choose to be peacemakers, the world recognizes us as coming from God and reflecting his likeness. To take up the mantle of *peacemaking* is to participate in and display the nature of God.

The other side of the coin is that when Christians are not committed to peacemaking, they reflect something other than the nature of God and are viewed with suspicion by the watching world. For example, it comes across as inconsistent when we call ourselves *pro-life*, but narrowly define *life* as unborn life in the womb. When Christians enthusiastically support military operations, the execution of criminals, and the torture of military prisoners, the pro-life mantra rings rather hollow. It becomes more "pro-this-life-but-not-that-life."

Let me remind you that I am not taking a position on the topics of warfare or capital punishment as government policies. That's a discussion for a different time and a different forum. My focus here is on the *hearts* of those who say they follow Jesus. Wars and executions should never bring a smile to the face of a true Christ follower. Such occasions should touch us deeply with mourning and remorse over our broken world, and should drive us to prayer for our nation and our world. The Bible says, "Don't rejoice when your enemies fall; don't be happy when they stumble" (Proverbs 24:17, NLT).

Looking back over the past decade of war in Afghanistan and Iraq, just imagine how different it might have been if tens of millions of evangelical Christians had spent time praying daily for members of al-Qaeda and the Taliban rather than tuning in to hours and hours of incendiary and cynical political talk radio, hosted by millionaire desk jockeys. For many evangelicals, that is a stomach-wrenching thought. But that is the sword of Jesus.

Jesus' days on earth were set against the backdrop of Roman power and occupation. Constant reminders of the domination of Caesar were a daily occurrence, with Roman soldiers milling in the streets, shaking down Jews for taxes, or forcing them to carry their gear for up to a mile at a time. It was clear to all Jews that Roman power and the Kingdom of God were incompatible. Israel was seething under the oppressive presence and domination of Rome, and a growing movement of Zealots was developing, looking to undermine the bully rulers, in the name of Jehovah.

That was the climate when Jesus arrived in the Holy City. And he came into the situation with weapons—but not the weapons of man. Jesus armed himself and his followers with techniques of cheek-turning, extra-mile-going, and cross-carrying.

As he came closer to Jerusalem and saw the city ahead,
he began to weep. "How I wish today that you of all
people would understand the way to peace. But now
it is too late, and peace is hidden from your eyes.

LUKE 19:41-42, NLT

Jesus wept over the attitude and posture of his Hebrew brethren. His heart broke over their failure to understand the ways
of peacemaking and how they had become peace-*blind*. Their
eyes were filled with visions of war and victory through violent means. Rather than being enraptured with the ways of
servanthood and the humility of the Cross, the people of
God were captive to the ways of domination. They had lost
the ability to envision methods of peace.

Jesus told Pilate, "My kingdom is not of this world. If
it were, my servants would fight" (John 18:36, NIV). He
certainly did not mean that his Kingdom would not be
manifested on earth, but rather that its *source* was not of
this world. Earthly kingdoms are established by the powerful through force and compulsion. Jesus preached and
practiced the establishment of his Kingdom through the
Cross, not the sword. His weapons were to overcome evil
with good, greed with giving, hatred with compassion, and
darkness with light. He sends us into the world armed in
the same way.

We need look no further than the last century to see that
peacemakers are the people who truly change the world.
Mahatma Gandhi, Nelson Mandela, Martin Luther King

Jr.—each had every reason imaginable to strike back in violent resistance. They each had many followers who would have willingly joined them in whatever means necessary. But they each chose the way of peace and suffering, rather than lashing out. They followed in the ways of peacemaking. Gandhi's doctrine and practice of nonviolence brought an end to the colonial rule of the British Empire in India. Nelson Mandela emerged from twenty-seven years of racist imprisonment with a redemptive posture that served to eradicate apartheid in South Africa. Dr. King's commitment to a civil rights movement that met terror and lynchings with nonviolent resistance changed American history.

To love a friend or a stranger or to regret the idea of human suffering is one thing. But to love an *enemy*, someone who has caused us harm or grief, is an altogether different matter. But "altogether different" is a trademark of the society that Jesus came to develop. "Altogether different" is the type of community he came to create and establish throughout the world.

A love big enough to encompass even our enemies is the kind of "altogether different" world-changing force that has proven effective time and time again. "Love *never* fails," writes the apostle Paul.[12]

When Jesus teaches us to love and to bless and to pray for our enemies, he is telling us he wants us to be "altogether different" from those who would respond with aggression and retaliation. He calls us to break the cycle of vengeance and hostility.

It is one thing to protect a child or a woman from the attacks of an abusive man. But to have mercy on the abuser, to pray with wholehearted fervor for him, and to visit him in prison is something altogether different. This is the mark of maturity that Jesus sets for us. This is actually loving our enemy through *peacemaking*. This is concrete Christianity . . . Christ following.

It is past time for evangelicals to revisit the New Testament idea of aggressive peacemaking, the peacemaking that Jesus taught. Our hearts must become disentangled from fear-driven pundits and political persuaders, who draw their wisdom not from heaven but from earthly ideologies. It is impossible to clench our fists while opening our hands. May we learn to weep over the things that make Jesus weep, and find our faith and joy in following him and his ways of peace.

Jesus calls us to the active task of peacemaking. It is not simply an *ideal* or a *doctrine* for mental assent. It is not an ethereal principle. Revangelicals are people who have moved from *believing* in peace to *behaving* in peace. Jesus brings down the sword of peace on our natural inclination to resort to violence and force. Peacemaking is neither a natural nor a neutral stance in the face of violence and broken relationships. But that's the point. When we enter into the blessedness of peacemaking, we demonstrate to the watching world that we are the offspring of God. And this is Good News that could only come from the Kingdom of Heaven.

QUESTIONS FOR REFLECTION

1. What do you believe about peace and peacemaking? What have your actions shown? Do you like peace when it's convenient, or do you *love* it (James 3:17) enough to help make it happen?

2. What would your life look like if you became a planter of seeds of peace with your words and actions?

3. In what ways are you personally challenged by the ideas of gospel peacemaking in this chapter? How does the sword of Jesus expose the division between your ways and God's ways?

9

REPOSITION

*Jesus . . . gave his charge: "God authorized and commanded
me to commission you: Go out and train everyone you
meet, far and near, in this way of life, marking them by
baptism in the threefold name: Father, Son, and Holy
Spirit. Then instruct them in the practice of all I have
commanded you. I'll be with you as you do this, day
after day after day, right up to the end of the age."*

MATTHEW 28:18-20, MSG

*This is a call for us to reconsider how we have been
approaching our life, in light of the fact that we
now, in the presence of Jesus, have the option of
living within the surrounding movements of God's
eternal purposes, of taking our life into his life.*

DALLAS WILLARD, *THE DIVINE CONSPIRACY*

GOD CHOSE followers of Jesus to be the newsboys and
newsgirls who stand on the streets announcing the "breaking news" that his reign has come . . . and it is good! His way
is the loving way of kindness, gentleness, humility, hope,
and joy. We are the Good News people. Let's act like it. The
hope for our world is not in the power and politics of a fallen
system born of the wisdom of humans. The only hope for

mankind lies in the in-breaking reign and rule of God—his Kingdom and the goodness it brings.

Christianity has lost home field advantage in America. But let's stop kicking the dirt and dropping our chins as if the game were over. Rather than lamenting the loss of a favored status in society, let us join the chorus of Jesus followers who are finding a new identity. Better yet, an *old* identity. Let us become revangelicals, the ones who are being rewired by the Good News of the Kingdom of Heaven and have beaten their swords into plowshares in order to bring restoration and renewal to a tired and worn-out world.

Let us join with others who have ceased to view non-Christians as enemies or evangelistic projects. Those who are so filled with faith in the power of the Good News of heaven that they are unwilling to be captivated by the fear of the bad news of earth. Revangelicals are believers who are rediscovering their Jesus heritage, embracing the transformative reality of serving over conquering; who are letting go of life—that is, of safety and security—to preserve and protect those things that are truly dear.

Revangelicals are embracing the challenge of a journey that draws them into the most radical, yet joyful, expression of Christianity they can imagine. They look at their neighbors as the frontline beneficiaries of the love of Christ.

Revangelicals like Laura Hairston, a young suburban housewife and mother of two little girls, have discovered a new identity and purpose. In the thriving city of Frisco, Texas (just north of Dallas), Laura and her husband, Ryan, began to lament that they had lived for several years in the same home but had few relationships with the people on their street. They began to ask, "How can we become *intentional* about reaching our neighbors? How can we be *Good News* in our neighborhood?"

After meditating on Jesus' metaphor of the Kingdom of Heaven being like yeast—which when mixed into a lump of dough mysteriously expands and moves through the entire lump, creating bread for food—Laura realized that starting small was okay; that she just needed to get involved somewhere, to get the yeast into the dough, so to speak.

She decided to join a morning exercise group, called Boot Camp, with some of the ladies in her subdivision. During one of their frequent coffee shop visits after a morning workout, one of the women in the group began to share her heartache about her middle-school daughter. She was having trouble getting her daughter to open up, and she said, "I wish there were someone who could mentor her or something."

Laura spoke up and said that she'd had a mentor at a similar age and she would love to reciprocate.

"Oh my gosh! You would do that for me?" the young mother said.

Laura assured her that it would be a joy for her to help out, and she began meeting with the daughter after school a couple of days a week. Before long, another middle schooler, the daughter of a single mom in the neighborhood, joined Laura's after-school mentoring table.

Word quickly spread among the Boot Camp moms,

several of whom approached Laura one by one, asking if their daughters could join the mentoring group. Before she knew it, Laura had more than half a dozen girls meeting in her home on Wednesday nights. After enjoying a meal together, they talk about their highs and lows of the week and Laura shares wisdom from the Bible that applies to their situations. Additionally, they work through a book, such as Jen Hatmaker's 7, about deciding to fight back against the modern-day diseases of greed, materialism, and overindulgence—an important topic for young girls growing up in an affluent city such as Frisco. Following that particular book study, the girls came up with the idea on their own to sponsor a World Vision child. The group recently began their third year of meeting together.

Laura Hairston is a revangelical. She is a Jesus follower who doesn't just point to weekly church attendance as proof of her devotion to him. She has personalized the call to go into all the world with the Good News of the Kingdom of Heaven, and she is convinced that "the world" begins in her subdivision. Laura's middle-school girls group is only one of many pieces the Lord has used in what has now become a church, started by the Hairstons out of their home.

If Jesus Meant What He Said

One Sunday afternoon, so the story goes, a little girl, the daughter of a pastor, tugged on her father's pant leg and asked, "Daddy, was what you were saying today true, or were you just preaching?" Maybe that actually happened somewhere, but I have heard so many pastors tell it as a first-person story that I can't be sure. Nevertheless, we find it humorous because too often it rings true. It has been observed, "Many of us praise Jesus' teachings as high ideals and then advocate a way to evade following them."[1]

The best way for us to become Good News people—revangelicals—is to take Jesus seriously. There is no truer litmus test for those who claim to love Jesus than to mix our actual lives with what he did and said:

> Jesus answered him, "If anyone loves me, he will
> keep my word, and my Father will love him, and we
> will come to him and make our home with him."
>
> JOHN 14:23

The key to abiding in Christ is obeying him. When we live and move in the words of Jesus, he lives and moves into our lives. Becoming a revangelical is a faith operation. Practicing the mercy and kindness we have looked at throughout this book does not come naturally to us. It comes through faith in Jesus, because we believe he knows what he's talking about. Our kind and merciful actions are rooted in the belief that not only is Jesus the Son of God, who looks into an open heaven, but also, from a human standpoint, he is the smartest person who ever lived. His heavenly heritage informs his ability as a human to say, "Live like this." That is the substance that moves us along as carriers of the Good News of the Kingdom of Heaven.

Gandhi said, "The message of Jesus as I understand it is contained in his Sermon on the Mount, unadulterated and taken as a whole; and even in connection with the Sermon on the Mount, my own interpretation of the message is different from the orthodox. The message, to my mind, has suffered distortion in the West."[2] The distortion Gandhi spoke of is largely due to the fact that we don't take Jesus seriously. Sure, we adhere to the convenient truths he preached; but when it comes to the inconvenient parts that press in on our earthly allegiances, priorities, and desires, we're more apt to sweep them under the rug by spiritualizing them rather than actualizing them.

When Christians remain fixated on protecting their own wealth and financial position, their own safety and security, and their own comfort and convenience, they remain on the outside, looking in at the Kingdom of Heaven, reduced to singing sentimental songs about the celestial world on "the other side." This mind-set rings hollow when compared to the requirements of total devotion to following Jesus and his ways. As Jesuit priest Avery Dulles writes:

The vocation to discipleship means a radical break from the world and its values. In the Synoptic Gospels, especially, we see discipleship as involving a total renunciation of family, property, income, worldly ambition, and even personal safety. The disciple, in the ideal case, forsakes all other security, making a total commitment to Jesus and the Kingdom.[3]

Revangelicals repledge their allegiance to the one and only Holy Nation. Favoring their citizenship in the Kingdom of Heaven, they seek to enter it and bring others in as well. The Kingdom of God is not something *we* build or establish. It is something we *enter into*. We receive it. It is God's realm. Its portal is obedience to the words and ways of Jesus. If we hope to experience God's peace, we commit to becoming peacemakers. If we desire to inherit the earth, we stop fighting for it. We commit to meekness rather than the use of power and supremacy. If we want to live in the realm of God's mercy, we become practitioners of mercy in our attitudes and actions.

My house has one of those little doggy doors on the back porch. It is just large enough for our smallest dog to get through. Living in Kansas City, we often eat at one of our favorite barbecue joints. When we've had some big beef ribs and bring the bones home for the dogs, one of them invariably tries to bring her bone into the house through the doggy door. But it's impossible. Still, she goes trotting up to the entrance with a huge bone in her mouth, and just as her nose passes through . . . bam! The bone catches each side of the entrance and she bounces back. She has to lay the bone down if she wants in. She can't bring it in with her.

The biggest problem we have with entering into the Kingdom of Heaven is that we try to take our stuff in with us. We try to assure our own means of sustainability, safety, and security. But we get stopped cold when we assume we can get into the Kingdom with our own agenda. Individualism, violence, judgment, and hoarding keep us from entering.

In pointed contrast to the kingdoms of men, which gain ascendancy by coercion and hierarchical power, Jesus' Kingdom is validated and expands by the power of love and compassion. That is the counterintuitive dynamic that inspires revangelicals to lay down our own rights and privileges each day. This is what it means to take up our cross *daily*.

Peter, James, and John were fishing partners. The first thing they did in order to follow Jesus was lay down their nets. Those nets represented their economic security, their livelihood, their purpose. Like my little dog and her bone, they couldn't get into the Kingdom of Heaven with their nets. Jesus told the rich young ruler, a young man accustomed to the lavish lifestyle of the economically elite, that he needed to sell everything he had in order to understand and show compassion to the poor. It was his lack of identification with the *least of these* that restrained this young man from entering into the joy of a fully engaged life of faith in God.

Jesus developed a core group of people who carried the DNA of the Kingdom of Heaven to the rest of the world. They not only brought the *word* of the Kingdom, they also delivered the substance of it. Revangelicals are Good News people who take the words of Jesus seriously. Their lives and faith communities are tangible good news to the people they encounter, and their collective witness is a light in their worlds. They are cities set on a hill in their neighborhoods and communities. Revangelicals are the Jubilee people in flesh and blood.

Eugene Peterson's paraphrase of Jesus' words in Matthew 5:13-16 serve as an apt description of Jesus' call to Revangelicals:

> Let me tell you why you are here. You're here to be salt-seasoning that brings out the God-flavors of this earth. If you lose your saltiness, how will people taste godliness? You've lost your usefulness and will end up in the garbage.
>
> Here's another way to put it: You're here to be light, bringing out the God-colors in the world. God is not a secret to be kept. We're going public with this, as public as a city on a hill. If I make you light-bearers, you don't think I'm going to hide you under a bucket, do you? I'm putting you on a light stand. Now that I've put you there on a hilltop, on a light stand—shine! Keep open house; be generous with your lives. By opening up to others, you'll prompt people to open up with God, this generous Father in heaven.[4]

Good news is welcomed by most everyone. In the heart of every Christian on the face of the earth is the Good News of the Kingdom of Heaven. Here's to the revangelicals, the Good News people who are bringing out the God-flavors of the earth and are shining translucent God-colors throughout the world by committing and faithfully representing the great name of Jesus Christ. Here's to the ones who have revisited the ways and means of Jesus and have tossed aside the methods and madness of earthly pursuits. Here's to those who have joined that great cloud of witnesses to live in testimony of the Good News of the Kingdom of Heaven.

Notes

CHAPTER 1: RECALIBRATE

1. The Romans Road is a widely used evangelism system, laying out a plan of salvation based on a progression of verses from the New Testament book of Romans. A typical "road" might include the following verses: Romans 3:23; 6:23; 5:8; 10:13; 10:9; and 8:1.

2. For those too young to remember, blue laws were statutes that limited or prohibited commercial activity on Sunday, which was a day set aside for worship and rest according to the biblical example of the Sabbath.

3. These points are congruent with David Bebbington's summary of a contemporary definition of modern evangelicalism. See www.nae.net /church-and-faith-partners/what-is-an-evangelical.

4. E. Stanley Jones, *Christ's Alternative to Communism* (New York: Abingdon, 1935), 130.

CHAPTER 2: REPENT

1. Erwin W. Lutzer, *Is God on America's Side? The Surprising Answer and How It Affects Our Future* (Chicago: Moody, 2008), 52.

2. Romans 1:16, NKJV

3. Luke 9:55, NASB

4. See Galatians 5:22-23.

5. 1 Corinthians 1:18

6. See Matthew 5:44.

7. Mark 9:23

8. Mark 9:24

9. See 1 Corinthians 3:9-15.

10. See Matthew 9:17.

11. This quote has been attributed to a variety of pundits and philosophers, including Voltaire, Jean-Jacques Rousseau, George Bernard Shaw, and, of course, Mark Twain. A version also appears in the 1955 play *Inherit the Wind* by Jerome Lawrence and Robert Edwin Lee.

12. Acts 9:4

13. Scot McKnight, *The King Jesus Gospel: The Original Good News Revisited* (Grand Rapids: Zondervan, 2011), 20.

14. John Ortberg, "Who Are the Experts on Life Transformation?" in Dallas Willard, *Living in Christ's Presence: Final Words on Heaven and the Kingdom of God* (Downers Grove, IL: InterVarsity, 2014), 45.

15. Matthew 6:10

16. These five points are adapted from the work of E. Stanley Jones, *Christ's Alternative to Communism* (New York: Abingdon, 1935), 41–42.

17. To find out more about JUSTembrace and how you can get involved in your local community, go to justembrace.org.

CHAPTER 3: RECOMMIT

1. Dallas Willard, *Renovation of the Heart: Putting On the Character of Christ* (Colorado Springs: NavPress, 2002), 238–239. Italics in the original.

2. Stuart Murray, *Post-Christendom: Church and Mission in a Strange New World* (Carlisle, UK: Paternoster, 2004), 83–84.

3. Michael Frost, *Exiles: Living Missionally in a Post-Christian Culture* (Peabody, MA: Hendrickson, 2006), 5.

4. Rush Limbaugh, "It's Sad How Wrong Pope Francis Is (Unless It's a Deliberate Mistranslation by Leftists)," transcript of *The Rush Limbaugh Show*, November 27, 2013, www.rushlimbaugh.com/daily/2013/11/27 /it_s_sad_how_wrong_pope_francis_is_unless_it_s_a_deliberate _mistranslation_by_leftists.

5. Igor Bobic, "Sarah Palin 'Surprised' by Pope Francis' 'Liberal' Sounding Statements," TPM LiveWire, November 12, 2013, http://talkingpointsmemo.com/livewire/sarah-palin-surprised -by-pope-francis-liberal-sounding-statements.

6. Ronald J. Sider, *The Scandal of Evangelical Politics: Why Are Christians Missing the Chance to Really Change the World?* (Grand Rapids: Baker, 2008), 19.

7. C. S. Lewis, *The Screwtape Letters* (1942), HarperCollins edition (New York: HarperCollins, 2001), 34–35.

8. Nicholas Kristof, "Where Is the Love?" The Opinion Pages, *New York Times*, November 27, 2013, www.nytimes.com/2013/11/28/opinion /kristof-where-is-the-love.html?_r=0. Italics added for clarity.

9. Gregory A. Boyd, *The Myth of a Christian Religion: Losing Your Religion for the Beauty of a Revolution* (Grand Rapids: Zondervan, 2009), 22. Italics in the original.

10. Ibid., 14.

11. Matthew 6:33

12. E. Stanley Jones, *Christ's Alternative to Communism* (New York: Abingdon, 1935), 164.

13. Dallas Willard, *The Divine Conspiracy: Rediscovering Our Hidden Life in God* (San Francisco: HarperSanFrancisco, 1998), 19–20.

14. Tom Krattenmaker, *The Evangelicals You Don't Know: Introducing the Next Generation of Christians* (Lanham, MD: Rowman & Littlefield, 2013), 107.

15. Ibid., 107–108.

16. Jonathan Merritt, *A Faith of Our Own: Following Jesus beyond the Culture Wars* (New York: FaithWords, 2012), 31.

17. Willard, *Divine Conspiracy*, 59. Italics in the original.

18. Glen H. Stassen, *Living the Sermon on the Mount: A Practical Hope for Grace and Deliverance* (San Francisco: Jossey-Bass, 2006), 18.

19. Ibid.

20. Boyd, *Myth of a Christian Religion*, 19.

21. N. T. Wright, *Surprised by Hope: Rethinking Heaven, the Resurrection, and the Mission of the Church* (New York: HarperOne, 2008), 184–185.

CHAPTER 4: RECONCILE

1. Matthew 11:19

2. Luke 10:30-32

3. John Wesley and John Emory, *The Works of the Reverend John Wesley, A.M.* (New York: J. Emory and B. Waugh, for the Methodist Episcopal Church, J. Collard, printer, 1831), 330–331.

4. 1 Corinthians 5:9-13, MSG. Italics in the original.

5. The Reverend Dr. Martin Luther King Jr., "Towards Freedom," a speech made at Dartmouth College, May 23, 1962, www.dartmouth.edu /~towardsfreedom/transcript.html.

6. See Matthew 25:34-45.

7. Bob Roberts Jr., *Bold as Love: What Can Happen When We See People the Way God Does* (Nashville: Thomas Nelson, 2012), 13. Italics in the original.

8. Luke 4:22

9. See Matthew 4:12-16.

10. John 8:7

11. Alan Hirsch and Debra Hirsch, *Untamed: Reactivating a Missional Form of Discipleship* (Grand Rapids: Baker, 2010), 238.

12. Richard Rohr, "The Sin of Exclusion," *Richard Rohr's Daily Meditations* e-mail, June 14, 2013.

13. See 1 Timothy 6:12.

CHAPTER 5: REPRESENT

1. John 20:21.

2. Michael Frost, *Exiles: Living Missionally in a Post-Christian Culture* (Peabody, MA: Hendrickson, 2006), 54-55. Italics in the original.

3. See "A Man Stole This Woman's Wallet, and You Won't Believe What Happened Next," *The Good News*, October 22, 2013, http://shine.yahoo .com/ellen-good-news/man-stole-woman-8217-wallet-won-8217-t -181400909.html; and "Everyone Matters," Facebook, October 30, 2013, http://m.facebook.com/story.php?story_fbid=433769000063097 &id=211695172270482.

4. Dan Kimball, *They Like Jesus but Not the Church: Insights from Emerging Generations* (Grand Rapids: Zondervan, 2007), 26.

5. "Dawkins Calls for Mockery of Catholics at 'Reason Rally,'" *Catholic News Agency*, March 27, 2012, www.catholicnewsagency.com/news/ dawkins-calls-for-mockery-of-catholics-at-reason-rally.

6. "'Nones' on the Rise," Pew Research Religion & Public Life Project, October 9, 2012, www.pewforum.org/unaffiliated/nones-on-the-rise.

7. Luke 10:26-27

8. Luke 10:29, MSG

9. Luke 10:36

10. Luke 10:37, MSG

11. Ibid.

CHAPTER 6: RENEW

1. Luke 4:19

2. E. Stanley Jones, *Christ's Alternative to Communism* (New York: Abingdon, 1935), 156.

3. "AFL-CIO Exposes Soaring CEO Salaries with Interactive World Map," *Union Plus*, April 25, 2013, http://www.unionplus.org/blog/union-issues /AFL-CIO-exposes-soaring-CEO-salaries.

4. Michael Hiltzik, "CEO-to-Worker Pay Gap Is Obscene; Want to Know How Obscene?" *Los Angeles Times*, October 20, 2013, http:// www.latimes.com/business/la-fi-hiltzik-20131020,0,770122. column#axzz2jPNa3Nhu.

5. See the website for Evangelicals for Social Action (ESA) at http://webcache
.googleusercontent.com/search?q=cache:vc76N9wiQioJ:www
.evangelicalsforsocialaction.org/embracingthefuture/social-change/+&cd=5
&hl=en&ct=clnk&gl=us.

6. Jones, *Christ's Alternative to Communism*, 163.

7. Mark 1:18, MSG

8. Luke 4:19, KJV

9. Jodi Garbison, interview with the author, September 5, 2013.

10. Alan Hirsch and Lance Ford, *Right Here, Right Now: Everyday Mission for
Everyday People* (Grand Rapids: Baker, 2011), 139.

11. Adelle M. Banks, "Poll: Nearly 80 Percent of Americans Say They Are
Christian," *Houston Chronicle*, January 5, 2012, www.chron.com/life
/houston-belief/article/Poll-Nearly-80-percent-of-Americans-say-they-are
-2444092.php.

12. Hirsch and Ford, *Right Here, Right Now*, 144.

13. Isaiah 58:12, NLT

CHAPTER 7: RESTORE

1. See Matthew 3:13-17; Mark 1:9-11; Luke 3:22.

2. Glen H. Stassen and David P. Gushee, *Kingdom Ethics: Following Jesus in
Contemporary Context* (Downers Grove, IL: InterVarsity, 2003), 41–42.
Some italics added.

3. This is verse 4, NLT. For a fuller description, read Isaiah 40:3-5.

4. Kurt Rietema, interview with the author, July 23, 2013.

5. See http://brehmcenter.com/initiatives/micahgroups/course/2013
/vision#preacher.

6. David Frum, "Conservatives, Don't Despair," *CNN Opinion*, November
13, 2012, http://www.cnn.com/2012/11/12/opinion
/frum-conservatives-despair.

7. Proverbs 17:5, NLT

8. Jack Jenkins, "Congressman's Misuse of Bible Verse Belies Bad Theology
and Ideology on Food Stamps," *ThinkProgress*, May 23, 2013, http://
thinkprogress.org/economy/2013/05/23/2053081/congressmans-misuse
-of-bible-verse-belies-bad-theology-and-ideology-on-food-stamps.

9. Matthew 13:22

10. Timothy J. Keller, *Generous Justice: How God's Grace Makes Us Just*
(New York: Dutton, 2010), 103.

11. Christopher Neiger, "Why Car Title Loans Are a Bad Idea," CNN.com
/living, October 8, 2008, www.cnn.com/2008/LIVING/wayoflife/10/08
/aa.car.title.loans/index.html?iref=newssearch.

12. "A Profile of the Working Poor, 2011," BLS Reports, US Bureau of Labor Statistics, April 2013, http://www.bls.gov/cps/cpswp2011.pdf.

13. Jeff Nall, "Lies of Plutocracy: Exploding Five Myths That Dehumanize the Poor," *Truthout*, October 26, 2012, www.truth-out.org/news/item/12264 -lies-of-plutocracy-exploding-five-myths-that-dehumanize-the-poor#V.

14. "Working But Still Poor," *The Week*, February 2, 2013, http://theweek .com/article/index/239499/working-but-still-poor.

15. "Big Business, Corporate Profits, and the Minimum Wage," NELP Data Brief, July 2012, http://nelp.3cdn.net/24befb45b36b626a7a_v2m6iirxb .pdf.

16. David Zeiler, "How the 'Wal-Mart Syndrome' Pushes Millions More onto Food Stamps," Money Morning, June 13, 2013, http://moneymorning .com/2013/06/13/how-the-wal-mart-syndrome-pushes-millions-more -onto-food-stamps/.

17. Travis Waldron, "Study: CEO Pay Increased 127 Times Faster Than Worker Pay Over Last 30 Years," ThinkProgress, May 3, 2012, http:// thinkprogress.org/economy/2012/05/03/475952/ceo-pay-faster -worker-pay/#.

18. "Working But Still Poor," *The Week*.

19. E. Stanley Jones, *Christ's Alternative to Communism* (New York: Abingdon, 1935), 27–28.

CHAPTER 8: REUNITE

1. Jim Lobe, "Conservative Christians Biggest Backers of Iraq War," *Common Dreams*, October 10, 2002, www.commondreams.org/headlines02 /1010-02.htm.

2. *Merriam-Webster's Collegiate Dictionary*, 11th edition, emphasis added.

3. See Matthew 7:12; Luke 6:31.

4. Johann Baptist Metz, *The Emergent Church: The Future of Christianity in a Postbourgeois World* (New York: Crossroad, 1981), 42.

5. Clarence Jordan, *The Substance of Faith and Other Cotton Patch Sermons* (New York: Association Press, 1972), 69.

6. William Hendriksen, *New Testament Commentary: Exposition of the Gospel According to Matthew* (Grand Rapids: Baker, 1973), 310. Italics in the original.

7. Matthew 5:39

8. Glen H. Stassen, *Just Peacemaking: Transforming Initiatives for Justice and Peace* (Louisville: Westminster/John Knox, 1992), 69.

9. See, for example, Matthew 11:15; Mark 4:9, 23; Luke 8:8; 14:35.

10. See Matthew 16:5-12.

11. Luke 12:51
12. See 1 Corinthians 13:8.

CHAPTER 9: REPOSITION

1. Glen H. Stassen, *Just Peacemaking: Transforming Initiatives for Justice and Peace* (Louisville: Westminster/John Knox, 1992), 33.
2. K. L. Seshagiri Rao, *Mahatma Gandhi and Comparative Religion* (Delhi: Motilal Banarsidass, 1978), 30.
3. Avery Dulles, *A Church to Believe In: Discipleship and the Dynamics of Freedom* (New York: Crossroad, 1982), 9.
4. Matthew 5:13-16, MSG

Acknowledgments

THE THOUGHTS EXPRESSED in this book are the outgrowth of countless contributions from friends, family, teachers, writers, circumstances, and events. It would be impossible to list all the wonderful men and women who have helped me in my ongoing attempts to grasp Jesus' message. But in the limited space I have here, I want to give thanks to the following people:

Stanley Jones, Glen Stassen, Dallas Willard, and Brennan Manning, for their prescient insights into the gospel.

The many visionaries I have discovered since I began this book journey—such as Brandan Robertson, Evangelicals for Social Action, and the Christian Community Development Association—who are moving to redefine what it means to be Good News people.

My grandparents, Guy and Iva Ford, who were the first gospel people in my life. Though you both have been gone for more than three decades, the aroma of your lives still permeates mine. I can't wait to see you again.

My editor, Dave Lindstedt. This book is far better because of you. I don't want to write again without your help.

My agent, Mark Sweeney. I will be forever grateful to you, my brother, for believing in this book with such passion. Your encouragement was priceless.

My tribe, Forge Mission Training Network. I searched for you half my life, and it was worth it.

Alan Hirsch and Michael Frost. Your influence in my life is immeasurable. You were my heroes and became my dear friends and big brothers.

My best friends in different seasons of life: Kevin Garrett, John Knox, Brad Brisco.

My son, Jordan, the person I wish I was more like.

Finally, Sherri. Strong as a rock, as beautiful as the morning.

About the Author

Lance Ford is a cofounder of the Sentralized conferences. With more than two decades of experience as a pastor and church planter, Lance is a writer, coach, and consultant who has designed unique training systems currently being used by networks, seminaries, and leaders throughout the world. His passion is to resource and equip churches and leaders as they develop lifestyles of living the mission of the gospel. Lance holds a master's degree in global leadership from Fuller Theological Seminary. He is the author of several books, including *Right Here, Right Now: Everyday Mission for Everyday People* (with Alan Hirsch), *UnLeader*, and *The Missional Quest* (with Brad Brisco). Lance serves on the national leadership team for the Forge America missional training network. He and his wife, Sherri, have three adult children.

For *Revangelical* videos, small group resources,
and more, visit revangelicalbook.com

Online Discussion *guide*

TAKE *your* TYNDALE READING EXPERIENCE *to the* NEXT LEVEL

A FREE discussion guide for this book is available at bookclubhub.net, perfect for sparking conversations in your book group or for digging deeper into the text on your own.

www.bookclubhub.net

You'll also find free discussion guides for other Tyndale books, e-newsletters, e-mail devotionals, virtual book tours, and more!